PERSONNEL LETTERS
READY TO GO!

Cheryl D. Wilson
Frank Barnett,
Consulting Editor

Printed on recyclable paper

NTC Business Books

a division of *NTC Publishing Group* • Lincolnwood, Illinois USA

While a great deal of care has been taken to provide accurate and current information, the ideas, suggestions, general principles and conclusions presented in this text are subject to local, state and federal laws and regulations, court cases and any revisions of same. The reader is thus urged to consult legal counsel regarding any points of law—this publication should not be used as a substitute for competent legal advice.

All names of individuals and companies used in this book are fictional. Any similarities with the names of individuals living or deceased or with the names of companies currently or previously in business are purely coincidental.

Library of Congress Cataloging-in-Publication Data

Wilson, Cheryl D.
    Personnel letters ready to go / Cheryl D. Wilson, Frank Barnett, consulting editor.
        p. cm.
    ISBN 0-8442-3542-3
    1. Communication in personnel management. 2. Form letters.
I. Barnett, Frank, 1933- . II. Title.
HF5549.5.C6W535 1995
    651.7'5--dc20   94-41439
                                                                 CIP

Published by NTC Business Books, a division of NTC Publishing Group
4255 West Touhy Avenue, Lincolnwood (Chicago), Illinois 60646-1975 U.S.A.
© 1995 by NTC Publishing Group.
Manufactured in the United States of America.

5 6 7 8 9 0 ML 9 8 7 6 5 4 3 2 1

CONTENTS

◆

PART II: SAMPLE LETTERS

Chapter 7: *Training and Career Development Letters* *96*

Chapter 8: *Restructuring, Downsizing and Layoff Letters* *108*

ACKNOWLEDGMENTS

◆

This book would not have been possible without the many contributions made by human resources professionals all across the country. Material was submitted by a variety of companies diverse in their size and the industries they represent. To the following individuals and organizations we would like to express our deepest appreciation: Brenda A. Duncan (Chicago, IL); Enterprise Leasing Company (Irving, TX); Futura Industries (Clearfield, UT); Skip Sperry, Compliance Attorney, IEC Management Resource Group (Boise, ID); Management & Training Corporation (Ogden, UT).

Many others were kind enough to share their best materials with us and we wish to express our gratitude to them as well. To protect the privacy of their employees and their firms, they have asked to remain anonymous.

Finally, our special thanks to the two law firms who contributed to our text: Wessels & Pautsch, P.C. (St. Charles and Chicago, IL; Milwaukee, WI; Davenport, IA) and Laner, Muchin, Dombrow, Becker, Levin & Tominberg, Ltd. (Chicago, IL). Wessels & Pautsch, P.C. represents management exclusively in labor and employment matters. They recently developed two labor and employment guides for management, *The Illinois Answer Book* and *The Wisconsin Answer Book*. Laner, Muchin, Dombrow, Becker, Levin & Tominberg, Ltd. concentrates in the representation of employers in labor relations, employment litigation, and employee benefit matters.

PART I: GETTING STARTED

◆

1

The Basics of Good Business Writing

The *American Heritage Dictionary of the English Language*, Third Edition, defines communication as "The exchange of thoughts, messages or information, as by speech, signals, writing or behavior." People in business, whatever their place on the organizational chart, spend a good part of each day involved in this exchange. The exchange may take a variety of forms. It may be a call to a vendor, a presentation to superiors, or an informal meeting with peers to discuss the latest gossip. In some exchanges the business person will be the sender; in others the recipient. But, whatever the role played, one thing is clear. Without the various bits and pieces that make up every exchange, most people in organizations would find it difficult to do their jobs.

THE COST OF POOR COMMUNICATION

Whenever there is an exchange, there is also the chance for misunderstanding and the transmittal of incorrect information. When this happens the reactions of the parties involved may range from bewilderment to frustration. Unless clarified, the verbal or written dialogue can easily lead to anger and the refusal to attempt any further exchange. Anyone who has ever worked in an office can tell you stories of warring departments or battling co-workers. The specifics may differ, but at the heart of each situation were people who stopped communicating and stopped listening.

Imagine this scenario. The HR department of *Perkins, Inc.*, has finalized the details for the company's annual picnic. The picnic is two weeks away and this year the HR department has outdone itself. A memo from HR goes out company-wide. In the most enthusiastic of tones, it tells the staff about the upcoming picnic and all they have to look forward to--the food, the games, the prizes. From the description, they should almost be able to smell the hot dogs and popcorn. Just one problem. The memo doesn't say **where** the picnic is being held. The result? Either someone in HR will be fielding a lot of calls, or more trees will perish when a second memo is sent out giving the picnic location and how to get there.

Miscommunication is costly to business. It means wasted time and ultimately wasted dollars. People who can express themselves well, both verbally and in writing, are sought after and highly prized. This one skill, the ability to communicate effectively, may well be the difference between business success and business failure--both for the individual and the organization.

The purpose of this book is to help you master one aspect of your communication responsibilities: letter writing.

THE FUNDAMENTALS OF GOOD BUSINESS WRITING

There may be no greater moment of panic for a businessperson than when faced with a blank sheet of paper or an empty computer screen and a pressing deadline. You wonder how you will ever be able to fill all that space. Further, when you *are* done, will it make any sense?

Writing by its very nature is difficult. Trying to string words together so they are clear and say what you mean is a true challenge. It can also be as back-breaking as working construction. No wonder otherwise competent people try to avoid the task altogether.

Contrary to popular belief, good writers aren't blessed by the Muses. They simply practice enough until it seems as if they are. Writing well can be learned. Good business writing, like anything else, doesn't simply "happen." It isn't a matter of luck or chance. It's based on something far less elusive and abstract. It's called planning.

STRATEGY FOR EFFECTIVE WRITTEN COMMUNICATION

When it comes to creating effective written communication, planning is as important as the actual writing. Long before a single word is written you should have a roadmap that shows how to get from Point A to Point B. That plan or strategy should be equally applicable to any writing assignment. It should work in developing a one-page letter, a 25-page proposal, or a 160-page book.

Step 1: Your Objectives

The first step in preparing for your writing trip is to decide what you wish to accomplish. What exactly is your goal or desired outcome? Are you writing to inform? To explain? To persuade? To request materials or a specific action?

Though your message may have one primary objective, it is likely it will also have one or more secondary purposes. You may begin by explaining something to the reader but end by asking him to do something. It may help you to focus your writing if you try to state in one sentence the purpose of your communication. Begin by listing the key goal first followed by any other intentions of lesser significance.

Step 2: The Means

After you have listed all the intents of your communication, you will have to select the best medium for their achievement. Here you should confirm that a written communication is genuinely appropriate. Often it may not be. A manager whose staff has been sparring with the staff of another department head may get a better response from a face-to-face meeting with the fellow manager. Sending yet another piece of paper could compound the problem or be met with an indifferent silence.

A phone call might also be a legitimate alternative to something in prose form. There is certainly no reason to invest the energy in developing a written communique if another option is more time and cost effective.

When to put it in writing. The speed of phone calls aside, there will be times when only something in writing will do. Business people in a negotiating situation, for example, would want a written record both to track the progress of the negotiation and to show what was agreed to and what remained unresolved. Among other things, written documents can provide the history of a project or chronicle why one course of action was decided upon instead of another. Further, the documents will still be available even if the writers are not.

Writing may also be a more convenient way to relay information when there are a large number of individuals involved and no way to bring them together. Finally, as Chapter 3 on documentation illustrates, written records may even safeguard an organization.

The best medium. Once you have determined that the written word is appropriate for what you wish to say, you must decide the form it will take. Should it be a letter? A report? Is a formal memorandum necessary if an E-mail message or fax can produce the same result and more quickly?

Selecting the "best" medium will largely be determined by your subject and whether the communication is for internal staff or outside parties. Generally, letters would go to those outside your organization, while memos would be sent internally. If your communication is describing a lengthy and complex problem, an E-mail message is probably not appropriate. A serious subject should be treated formally; a mundane topic can be given a more matter-of-fact treatment.

What you say and how you say it depends on whom you are communicating with and the relationship you share. This leads to the next stage in our communication strategy.

Step 3: Your Reader

Who is your reader? You will certainly have a greater chance for communication success if you know who you are writing to. Your audience will determine the content of your message, the approach used, and even the tone of the message. An accountant, for example, could use terminology in a report to another accountant that he/she couldn't use in writing to someone who doesn't have a financial background. To such a person "GAAP" (generally accepted accounting principles) may mean nothing more than a place to buy jeans.

Knowing your reader allows you to tailor your message for maximum impact and understandability. Here are some general guidelines you may wish to follow to make sure your messages are appropriate for your audience:

1. Write to the knowledge level of your readers. If they are not technical types, avoid jargon, acronyms, or other "alphabet soup" that will get in the way of your meaning.

2. Decide how much detail is needed. If you are writing the 99th memo on a subject, it shouldn't be necessary to recap everything that has happened since Memo #1.

3. Personalize your writing so each reader feels you are speaking directly to him or her. Be professional, yet cordial.

4. Write from the readers' perspective. Show why your message should be of interest to them or how they will benefit by following your recommendations.

5. Avoid language that could be interpreted as sexist, racist or in other

ways discriminatory. It is unlikely that readers offended by your message will respond at all, let alone do anything you have asked.

6. Use the proper tone. Correspondence to a superior would be more formal than correspondence on the same topic to a peer.

Step 4: Collecting the Facts

Once you have outlined your objectives and evaluated your audience, the next step is to collect the information needed to make your message complete and factually correct. If you are making a recommendation to a committee, for example, you should include data that supports the course of action you are suggesting. That data could be projected benefits expense or the results of a salary survey. Resolving a complaint that has been ongoing for several months might involve reviewing any notes or earlier correspondence on the subject. A second step would be to speak with any individuals familiar with the matter to pinpoint specific obstacles to resolution. If you have been asked to write a proposal but have never done one before, you would seek out one or more people with experience in the area and ask their advice. You might also request examples of their proposals to use as models.

For more complex writing assignments, the information available within the company may not be enough. In these cases outside resources are necessary. Finding what you need could be as simple as a quick trip to the local library. Other research tools you might use, if the project warranted, are customer surveys, one-on-one client interviews, focus groups (meetings with key clients and/or potential clients to discuss specific issues), long-term studies and consultations with outside firms. One or a combination of these more sophisticated methods will help you uncover the facts you need.

While you're gathering facts, you should also be brainstorming about what will go in the actual document you are going to produce. Jot down ideas as they come to you. Build on the objective lists you began at the start of the assignment. Write down what you want to get across, perhaps even putting down key phrases you wish to include in your correspondence. Outline all the points you want to be sure to cover. Try to foresee objections so you can counter them in your message. All this preliminary work will pay off when you begin to write.

Step 5: The First Draft

Armed with objectives, all relevant data, and an outline or list of points to cover, you are ready to begin your first draft. At this stage your only concern should be getting your thoughts down, either on paper or on disk. During this phase you needn't worry about spelling, punctuation or other mechanics. Polishing and refining will come later. Coherence isn't even important. It is quite acceptable to write sections out of sequence. If one part is easier to approach than another, then do it first. It is not unusual for the body of a document to be written before the beginning or the end. Knowing what to say in the middle is often easier than knowing how to start or close.

Remember that you don't have to share anything you write now. It doesn't have to be perfect. You are free to make additions, deletions, move paragraphs, etc. Knowing you will have the opportunity to revise your work should keep your anxiety to a minimum. If you are faced with something that is especially difficult to express, tackle something else and return to the complicated material later. Simply keep the words flowing.

One way to keep the words coming is to pretend you are actually talking to your reader. What would you say if he or she were seated across the table from you? How would you make sure your message is understood? Counter objections? Handle a negative response? Writing from this vantage point should help you achieve clarity and conciseness in your correspondence. Your letters and memos should also sound more natural. When you write as if you are speaking, you will be more aware of language that sounds overly formal, stilted or ambiguous and can keep it out of your documents. Note that this doesn't mean the language should be too informal. Slang or obscenities, for example, would be quite inappropriate. Standard English should give you more than enough ways to express yourself powerfully, persuasively and colorfully.

Following are a few ideas to help you develop your rough drafts:

1. Try to write quickly. You are more likely to get out everything you need to say if you don't worry too much about how to say it. Now isn't the time for pain-staking detail or long searches for the ideal words and phrases.

2. Use simple language that says what you mean. Express ideas clearly and succinctly. In general, keep sentences and paragraphs short. Avoid overly long and complex sentences.

3. Enhance the readability of your material by choosing words that are familiar and descriptive. Precise words create a more accurate picture in the reader's mind than words that are vague. For example, saying that a mini-van "comfortably seats eight" creates a stronger visual image than describing the same mini-van as "roomy."

4. Avoid cliches. These trite expressions will rob your writing of its personality and power.

5. As tempting as it may be, complete your first draft before going back to revise and edit it. There is an old writing expression: "Don't get it right, get it written." Sound advice. Once you have something to work with, you can tinker with it as much as you like. But, you can't fix what you haven't done.

6. Once finished, set the first draft aside at least for a few hours. If you have time, put it away for several days. It will be easier to catch mistakes, missing information, inconsistencies and other necessary corrections if you wrap up your work then return to it with a fresh eye.

Step 6: Revising Your Work

With the first draft finished you are now ready for the final phase of the writing process: revising your work. This stage gives you one last chance to perfect your material.

Most revisions include three activities: revising, editing and proofreading. Here is where details definitely count.

Revising. The revision process begins by taking a critical look at the first draft. The draft must be assessed on several levels. In terms of content, for example, how well does the material reflect the objectives you developed at the project's outset? Have you presented everything on your outline or list of key points and covered it in sufficient depth? Is your message clear? Have you written from your reader's point of view? Is the material well organized? Have you verified the accuracy of your facts and included all relevant supporting data? Is the physical layout of your document easy to follow?

Once you've identified weaknesses in the draft, you can usually correct them through rewrite and reorganization. If the document doesn't flow well, you can strengthen the transitions so there is a more logical progression from one idea to the next. Missing information can be added; sections that are well written but poorly placed can be moved where they will fit better. Awkward phrases may either be deleted or reworked.

To gauge the material's clarity and readability, consider asking someone else to review it. Such feedback could prove invaluable, particularly if the person is familiar with the matter discussed in your document and your reader(s). She/he may be able to highlight passages that ramble or confuse. As important, this audience of one can tell you how well you make your points or if your arguments and explanations are unconvincing. Use their advice to polish your final piece.

Editing. When the draft has been revamped to your satisfaction, you are ready to begin editing. Spelling, punctuation and grammar should be checked and any errors corrected. This is the time to eliminate redundancies and make sure you have made the proper word choices. For these tasks a good dictionary and thesaurus are indispensable tools.

If you are working on a computer that has spelling and grammar checking functions, use them. However, remember that the computer isn't infallible. You should still edit the material manually.

Proofreading. Before you distribute your memo throughout the company or send a letter to that important client, proofread it! This is truly the final opportunity to catch typos or other mistakes. Again, a spell checker is helpful, but it can't pick up the fact you typed in "and" when you really meant "an" or "manger" for "manager." It also won't point out word omissions.

Sending out a document with spelling and grammatical errors in it is not only embarrassing, it can lessen your credibility with your reader. It can convey the mistaken impression that you are careless or not very good with details. After taking the time to develop and revise a document, it's foolish not to take the last step to make sure it's right.

Final Recommendations. Here are some final thoughts on refining your materials before sending them out the door:

1. Aim for brevity. Always try to convey your message in the fewest possible words. This will add to the clarity of your correspondence since it won't be cluttered with excess verbiage.

2. Keep sentences simple by emphasizing only one or two ideas in each. If you try to include too much information, some of it is sure to get lost. Generally, the longer a sentence, the more difficult it is to follow.

3. A sentence that expresses the main idea or thought in a paragraph is called a topic sentence. Use these key sentences to introduce or summarize the most important information or facts in your material.

4. Like sentences, keep paragraphs the "right" length. Use your judgment here. Paragraphs should be long enough so they don't

seem choppy or abrupt, but short enough so they will actually be read. A page filled with line after line of dense, unbroken type is like asking your reader to find her way through a maze. Make sure the paragraphs tell what needs to be told, but give your reader a break by organizing the information in small bites on a page with plenty of white space.

5. Use the opening to "hook" your reader. Provide a reason compelling enough for them to read the entire document.

6. In the body of the document tell readers only what they need to know. Don't bog them down in unnecessary detail or repeat information they already know. Make your points and, if appropriate, show how they will benefit.

7. Close your correspondence by summarizing the document's purpose or main points. Conclude by clearly stating what you wish the reader to do.

One final bit of advice is to give yourself enough time to write and revise your correspondence. Putting something off until the last minute only increases the prospect of failure. Of course tight deadlines are sometimes unavoidable. In those instances you may have to compromise and settle for "good enough."

This six-step strategy provides an excellent framework for producing effective communications. Apply it consistently and you will complete your writing assignments more efficiently. What is more important, you will create clear, well-written correspondence that gets the desired results. One day you may even find yourself looking forward to the opportunity to put your thoughts on paper.

When your colleagues begin to describe you as one of those "natural born writers," smile and accept the compliment. No one has to know your ability to organize and present material is the result of a good formula and practice, and not just the touch of the Muses.

2

Good Human Resources Communication

The techniques that make any business correspondence effective are equally relevant to the materials written by human resources professionals. In human resources communications, as in all business writing, clarity is the key objective. Yet being clear is not enough. How things are said and how they are presented may be of even greater concern to those in HR. Individuals in this area often handle matters that are sensitive and confidential. Saying the wrong thing in print might not be fixable with an apology. As the examples in Chapter 3 will show, seemingly innocent statements in correspondence can have explosive consequences.

In a situation that is particularly touchy, the savvy HR professional will have any correspondence reviewed by corporate counsel before sending it to its addressee. The purpose of this chapter is to discuss the more typical correspondence written on a day-to-day basis, such as rejection letters, general company memos and the like.

TONE

The emotional quality of your correspondence is its tone. "Proper" tone will be dictated by the content of your correspondence, your relationship with the person or persons it is being sent to, and the effect or impact you wish the material to have. A solemn subject would have a somber tone and something of a more routine nature would have a neutral tone. Formality would be required--and expected--in a report to your company's board of directors. Humor would be apropos in a memo recapping the company picnic. In a letter to a promising candidate for whom there is currently no opening, you might aim to convey warmth, interest and the sense that there is genuinely an opportunity to join the firm in the future. Conversely, in a warning letter to an employee, the tone would reflect the seriousness of the offense and make it clear that change is necessary and must be immediate.

Words have the power to evoke images that are very potent and very real. Choosing words with precise shades of meaning will help your communication elicit the desired response from your readers. Using emotionally charged words or phrases, such as *suspension, final warning* and *termination*, may actually motivate a poor employee to improve his performance or change unacceptable conduct. Seeing such language in black and white for the first time is certain to rouse a strong visceral reaction.

You must be careful, however, not to include language in your correspondence that will send an unintended message or cause the recipient to respond in a way that will be harmful to the company. For example, if an unqualified candidate applies for a position, a politely worded rejection letter might disappoint him. On the other hand, a letter that bluntly states he would never be offered a job with your company, even if it meant world peace, could needlessly damage your company's reputation. The inflammatory letter would, of course, enrage the applicant and justifiably. It would be safe to bet that he would eagerly and angrily tell others of his negative experience with your organization. The image of your company could be tarnished and he may keep someone who would be an asset to you from considering your firm as a desirable place of employment.

PASSIVE VOICE

Throughout your academic career your teachers probably spent lots of time telling you to use active voice. Active voice, they may have explained, shows action and gives your writing color, vibrancy and movement. In sales, PR or promotional materials those characteristics would be particularly attractive. In certain human resources communications, though, active voice will sound harsh, cold and accusatory.

For any business writing relating to sensitive issues, passive voice has a number of virtues. In active voice, the action is performed by the subject of the sentence. In the passive, the subject is acted upon. This indirect construction is perfect for situations where tact and diplomacy are requisite. Let's go back to the scenario of the unqualified job candidate. If you were this person which letter would you prefer:

Active: *Dear Mr. Henderson:*

> *We have evaluated your application and concluded that your skills are inadequate for our opening.*

or

Passive: *Dear Mr. Henderson:*

> *Your application has been carefully evaluated. Unfortunately, your qualifications do not meet the criteria established for this position.*

As you can see, the passive voice is ideal for softening the blow of bad news, presenting negative information or placing the focus on the reader rather than the writer. It is also the right choice for communication that must be objective and impartial. Active voice can make communication seem biased.

ORGANIZING AND PRESENTING YOUR INFORMATION

How you organize the information in your correspondence will depend on what you have to say. Simply put, you would generally have one approach for information that is positive and another for negative information.

The Direct Approach

In routine letters or memos that are positive or neutral in tone, you will want to get right to the point. Here you would use a direct approach. In these cases you would state the most important fact at the beginning of your letter or memo. The main fact would then be followed by any supporting details or explanations. This approach works well in situations where the news is good. Someone who has gone through a grueling series of interviews would appreciate being told she got the job at the letter's outset. The direct approach is also effective in instances where the correspondence doesn't ask the recipient to do anything or requests something relatively easy (such as completing a brief form and returning it in an envelope that has been provided).

The Indirect Approach

When you have unpleasant news to relay, an indirect approach is a better way to present your information. Here, again, is where the passive voice comes in handy. With an indirect approach, you would first build a case then conclude by revealing your decision or action to the reader. Let's say, for example, you have to do a company-wide memo telling employees their health insurance premiums are going to increase by 15% in January. Rather than start out with this fact, which will most likely be met with groans and grumbles, you might begin by explaining you have had a larger percentage of claims this year than in previous years, as a result the insurance carrier has raised the company's rates, etc. As they read the memo, the employees will know what's coming. However, by presenting your case step-by-step, you have given them reasons to understand and accept the coming increase.

There are certain situations where the indirect approach should not be used to shield the reader. The shock value of the direct approach is more fitting and desirable. In correspondence relating to misconduct or other disciplinary matters, for example, information must be presented in a strong, direct, no-nonsense fashion.

3

Legal Aspects of HR Communication and the Importance of Documentation

LEGAL RAMIFICATIONS OF HR COMMUNICATION

Every time a human resource professional writes a letter to an employee or a potential employee, there is the opportunity for faulty communication. The legal impact of that miscommunication may come back to haunt the company. The following statements are just a few illustrations of potential problems:

1. *As long as you continue to do well, you will always have a job with us.* This statement goes right to the core of the employment–at–will relationship. Courts have ruled that statements like this constitute an "implied contract" of employment. Once an implied contract exists, employment is no longer "at will," and the employer is no longer free to terminate the employee with or without cause.

2. *Our situation does not mesh well with your personal needs.* This statement from a dismissal letter cost an employer more than $200,000. The employee being dismissed had returned to work following surgery for a malignant brain tumor. When he returned to work, he asked for and received approval to drop twenty percent of

---

Most of the information in this section was contributed by Wessels & Pautsch, P.C.. Wessels & Pautsch is a law firm that represents management exclusively in labor and employment law matters. The firm maintains offices in St. Charles and Chicago, Illinois; Milwaukee, Wisconsin; and Davenport, Iowa.

The Employment Writing Checklist at the end of the chapter was developed and contributed by Skip Sperry, Compliance Attorney with IEC Management Resource Group. IEC is a human resources consulting association based in Boise, Idaho. It serves over 800 employers throughout the Pacific Northwest.

his workload, with a corresponding reduction in salary. Four months later, he was fired.

Shortly before the employee's termination, he received a call from management encouraging him to work more hours. Then, his employer sent him a dismissal letter that included the above sentence.

This matter was settled by the employer agreeing to pay the ex–employee $200,000 to reinstate the employee in a new job and to train all of its managers in the employment provisions of the *Americans with Disabilities Act.*

3. *Your salary will be $20,000 per year.* Courts have held that this statement implies an employment contract because the employee's salary was expressed as a yearly figure. To avoid this pitfall, quote salary in terms of a weekly or a monthly figure.

4. *You will receive a performance review every December.* This statement certainly seems innocuous. The danger lies in the company's failure to live up to the "promise" it contains. A better statement might be, "You will receive an annual performance review." This does not commit the company to reviewing the employee during a specific month and reduces the chance that a court will construe "every" to mean "every year into the future."

5. *You will be paid $10.00 per hour.* If this statement is made to an independent contractor, it may be interpreted as establishing an employer/employee relationship.

Communications with independent contractors should be worded to strengthen, rather than call into question, the working relationship between the independent contractor and the firm. For example, payment should be by the job (not by the day, hour or other measure of time) and should be described as "contract payment." Instead of "discharge," refer to "contract termination."

6. *Our medical review officer has indicated to us that you are at increased risk for back injury.* A statement like this in a follow–up letter to a job applicant who has taken a post–offer physical examination can cause serious problems for the company. The applicant who is denied a job solely on the basis of "increased risk" of injury may well succeed in proving discrimination under the *Americans with Disabilities Act.*

   The ADA prohibits an employer from relying on "increased risk" of injury as a basis for its refusal to hire. The ADA mandates that the employer must look at whether the applicant is able to perform the duties of the job.

7. *We look forward to a long and prosperous future together.* What may appear to be no more than a pleasant way to close an offer letter could lead to major complications for the employer. Alluding to a "long future," according to the courts, creates an implied contract of employment and, consequently, eliminates an employment–at–will relationship.

8. *While you are on leave, the Company will pay your health insurance premiums for you.* A company that wishes to extend this offer to a valued employee should be aware of the following legal pitfalls. The offer cannot be restricted only to valued employees. The company must be prepared to make the **same** offer to **all** "similarly situated" employees, or risk the real likelihood of an employee lawsuit charging "disparate treatment." Note that, for purposes of leaves of absence, the courts have found pregnancy to be the same as other medical conditions (for example, heart attacks and back injuries).

   If the company offers to pay the employee's insurance premium, it should nevertheless provide the employee with a COBRA notice. Otherwise, the company may be sued for failure to furnish a COBRA notice and may find itself "on the hook" for sizeable medical bills.

As these statements show, imprecise or careless wording in business correspondence can do far more than confuse. It may also create binding contracts and other legal commitments that were not intended. A company may lose thousands of dollars as the result of these unintentional legal obligations, either in payment to employees who sue successfully or in legal fees as the company defends itself against the lawsuits.

Knowing that their writing may one day be presented as evidence in a courtroom, HR professionals must be particularly cautious of the things they commit to paper. The employment writing checklist at the end of the chapter may help you avoid common errors that could translate into major headaches for you and your company.

THE IMPORTANCE OF DOCUMENTATION

In addition to being careful in written exchanges, a company may also safeguard itself by accurately chronicling events as they happen. Documentation is an essential element to any human resources program. Every company should have a system in place whereby performance evaluations, employee disciplinary actions and any unusual occurrences are summarized in writing and filed for later use in justifying employment decisions and discipline.

Why document events that occur in the workplace? First, and most obvious, people simply cannot remember everything that goes on from day to day. Also, depending on the particular situation, there are specific reasons why documentation is a useful tool. Important among the reasons for documentation is the obvious potential for litigation in today's society. There is a tendency for courts and governmental agencies to apply the principle of: "If it isn't in writing, it didn't happen."

WHEN TO DOCUMENT

Following are some of the most common events that should be documented:

1. When a company is interviewing applicants for a new position, the company may wish to generate documents that show the reasons why certain employees who were interviewed were not hired.

2. When an employee is initially hired by the company, the company may wish to ask the employee to acknowledge in writing, if applicable, that he or she has been provided a handbook and has read and understands the handbook or has been explained company policies and understands them.

3. When the company hires a new employee, the company should generate a document, if applicable, stating that the employee has received certain company property.

4. During the term of employment, the company should document the following:

-   specific instances of performance that does not meet expectations (such as failure to meet production levels or insubordination) and performance that exceeds expectations;
-   specific instances of rule or policy violations;
-   all scheduled employee appraisals or reviews;
-   any conversation between a supervisor and an employee regarding work performance and any disciplinary action(s) taken in response;
-   dates and reasons (if provided by the employee) of lateness and absence; and
-   conversations regarding injuries on the job (to be filed in the employee's workers' compensation file).

5. After an employee appraisal or after disciplining an employee, the company may want to give the employee a chance to respond in writing. A written employee response serves as good evidence that

the appraisal or discipline did occur and was discussed with the employee.

In addition, when given the chance to respond, employees may feel as though they have been dealt with more fairly.

6. Upon an employee's separation from employment, the company should document the reason for the separation from employment. If the employee voluntarily left or quit a position, the company may want to obtain a statement from the employee stating that the separation from employment was indeed voluntary.

If an employee is discharged from employment, the potential is high for the discharged employee to file some sort of complaint against the company. Therefore, extreme caution must be taken to document carefully the circumstances surrounding the separation from employment. If an employee is terminated because of poor performance and/or rule violations, the company must be sure to document:

- the specific incidents giving rise to the employee's termination;
- witnesses to the specific incidents giving rise to the termination;
- the specific exchange of conversation that occurred when the employee was notified of his or her termination and the persons present at this time; and
- statements made by others with knowledge of the events giving rise to the termination.

HOW TO DOCUMENT

Following are a few suggestions for effective documentation:

1. *Document as soon as possible after the event.* Documents made immediately after the event may be viewed as more credible by a court or agency because it is more likely that a document made immediately after the event is more accurate than one that is made days or weeks later.

2. *Be as specific as possible.* In documenting each event be sure to include: what happened, where it happened, when it happened, who was there and who said what. Include everything that happened or was said. It is more important to "over include" than to "under include." Be as accurate as possible.

3. *Have a system for filing documents.* Decide whether documents are to be placed in each employee's personnel file or will be kept according to the type of document (for example, all performance appraisals are kept together, all employee acknowledgments of receipt of handbooks are kept together, etc.).

4. *Educate supervisors on documenting.* This will ensure that all relevant events are documented.

DOCUMENTING EMPLOYEE PERFORMANCE

Documentation of employee performance is helpful in charting an employee's development and in determining which employees should be promoted, given a raise, discharged, etc. If an employee calls the company's decisions into question by filing a discrimination charge or makes other allegations of unlawful conduct, documentation of employee performance may help the company to prevail in the subsequent charge or lawsuit.

Documentation of employee performance is also helpful at employee review periods. When instances of poor performance have been documented, a supervisor can point to the specific incidents such as attendance, conduct, etc., during the review and explain to the employee how his or her performance did not meet expectations.

DOCUMENTING DISCIPLINARY ACTION

Proper documentation of disciplinary action is vital. It establishes a record that may be helpful to the employer in various ways. Following are some of the benefits of documenting disciplinary action:

1. Documenting disciplinary actions enables the employer to determine whether the employee has received prior disciplinary action for a particular violation and what form of disciplinary action the employee received. The company can then determine the appropriate form of disciplinary action for any subsequent offenses.

2. Documentation of disciplinary action gives the company a mechanism for studying precedents when an employee engages in the same or similar types of conduct that have resulted in discipline for other employees.

3. Documentation of disciplinary action provides the essential "paper trail" when a company is forced to respond to a claim of unlawful conduct by an employee or former employee.

4. Documentation of disciplinary action may be helpful at equal employment opportunity hearings where an employee is alleging that termination, failure to promote or other employment action was due to discrimination on the company's part. In these cases, it is crucial that the company show that the employment action was not taken because of the former employee's sex, race, age, etc. as alleged, but was taken because of the employee's job performance. Extremely important in these situations are documents showing deficiency in employee performance, documents that indicate the company's efforts taken to counsel the employee, records of disciplinary action(s) taken and records of discussions at the termination meeting.

5. Documentation of disciplinary action may be helpful at unemployment insurance hearings. If, for example, the company protests a former employee's claim for benefits because the employee engaged in misconduct, documentation of employee performance appraisals or the circumstances surrounding the separation from employment may be useful.

DOCUMENTING EMPLOYEE MISCONDUCT

Listed below are a few guidelines for effective documentation of employee misconduct:

1. Document every disciplinary event and counseling session promptly, while events are fresh in mind. Handwritten dated notes are acceptable. Write as complete a story as possible, providing exact dates, times, places and conversations.

2. Record job–related standards and behaviors, not subjective interpretations. For example, instead of noting such behavior as "chronic absenteeism," record facts : "absent 4 days during December." Remember that speculation such as "He's probably been drinking again" should not be included in the file.

3. Focus on major issues related to performance and/or conduct and ignore minor issues.

4. Be sure to record the employee's side of the story during counseling or discipline sessions. This will document that the employee obtained a proper hearing and will insure that the employee's account does not change later.

5. In "final warnings" and other major disciplinary actions, make sure the employee reads and signs or initials the written record of the infraction and disciplinary action taken. If possible, have a second managerial or supervisory representative present at the meeting with the employee.

6. Avoid documentation that gives the appearance of "building a case" against an employee. It is best to let the record reflect an honest attempt to salvage the troubled employee. Otherwise, the employer may be propelled into court by an employee claiming "retaliatory discharge" or a "predetermined decision to fire."

7. Be careful to record similar violations in the same terminology. The employer needs to be able to show other employees were disciplined for similar offenses in a like manner. For example, when two employees are disciplined for refusing to perform a job, it would be unwise to describe the one employee's behavior as "unsatisfactory performance" and the other employee's action as "insubordination." In this instance, it would be best to record "refused to perform" for both cases.

See Exhibit B at the end of this chapter for a sample disciplinary documentation form. For employers, the bottom line of sound documentation of employee misconduct is to promote fairness and consistency.

DISCIPLINE AND THE "IMPOSSIBLE EMPLOYEE"

One of the most sensitive problems in the workplace is the problem employee. All efforts at using good supervisory skills have failed. Often there are overtones of threatened litigation.

An "impossible employee" may make vague references to "his attorney." Perhaps he has already filed a discrimination charge or has workers' compensation litigation going.

The problem employee makes clear by his behavior that he is no longer interested in cooperating with his employer. In this situation, a "firm but fair" warning letter may be very effective.

See Exhibits C and D at the end of this chapter for sample "firm but fair" warning letters. Letters like these have proven successful and are offered as models.

A human resource professional preparing such a warning letter should remember that the letter may someday become public knowledge. The letter should be written so that, if it were shown to a judge, a jury or government investigator, it would not cause the employer any concern. Indeed, it will be helpful.

Finally, keep in mind that the facts of the particular employment situation dictate the proper means of expression. When in doubt, contact the company attorney!

NOTE: The material contained in this chapter has been abridged from a variety of sources and is not necessarily applicable to a particular situation. The contents of this chapter should not be construed as legal advice. Readers should consult with legal counsel before taking any action on matters covered in this chapter.

EXHIBIT A

EMPLOYMENT WRITING CHECKLIST

This checklist provides an illustrative list of some common pitfalls to avoid when writing on behalf of your company. The list does not provide an exhaustive list of legal considerations, and various state laws may limit or void some of the ideas which follow. Please check your state's law before relying on any of these suggestions.

☐ Avoid terms of duration when describing employment, such as: *permanent* employee; salary of $35,000 *per year;* Welcome to the ABC, Inc., *family.* This will help preserve your at-will relationship.

☐ Avoid terms that would indicate a future dissolution of the employment at will relationship like *probation.* Courts have indicated that this term can cause employees to reasonably believe that after they are off probation, they have gained security in their positions. Substitute **introductory period** and **orientation period**. For disciplinary actions, use **immediate and sustained improvement**.

☐ Avoid unnecessarily binding your company with words like *must*, and *will.* Substitute permissive language such as **may, might**, etc.

☐ Avoid words of promise or guaranty. Rather than saying "Employees will have an *annual* review," substitute terms like **periodic, as warranted**, and **as needed.**

☐ Do not make lists, especially lists of disciplinary offenses, inclusive. Explain that the list is illustrative, not exhaustive.

☐ Write only what your are committed to doing. Don't unknowingly place additional requirements on your company. For example, do not include marital status in your EEO statement if it is not required by your state law unless your company wants to make that commitment.

EXHIBIT A

EMPLOYMENT WRITING CHECKLIST (CONTINUED)

☐ Use clear and concise language in your documents. Courts will construe ambiguous terms and conditions against the party who wrote the language.

— Avoid using legalese, especially in documents that perform a quasi-legal function (policies dealing with EEO, affirmative action, etc.).   The temptation to use legalese increases when you write about an area where compliance with the law is an issue, but try to stick to language that will be readily understood even by the untutored reader. If you must use certain legal terms, define them and relate them directly to your audience and the action they should take.

— Use everyday language. Eliminate excess verbiage and avoid innuendo. In other words, say what you mean and say it in as few words as you can without omitting vital information.

☐ Find third parties to read your documents and tell you what they think the document indicates and implies.

☐ Include an appropriate at-will disclaimer in any documents that could conceivably be construed as promises or contracts. Place at-will disclaimers in prominent positions and ensure they are conspicuous (use bold type, larger typeface, etc.).

☐ When drafting documents that will be distributed to employees, indicate that the company reserves the right to modify, change, amend, supplement, rescind or append the contents, but any changes must be in writing and signed by management. The documents cannot be changed orally by any employee.

☐ If the document is important and may have legal implications, consult your company's employment lawyer or association.

EXHIBIT B

Disciplinary Action Documentation Form

_____ Written Warning _____ Termination

Employee's Name _____

Department _____

Social Security # _____

Job Assignment _____

Problem: (What did the employee do or fail to do? When?)

_____
_____
_____

Discussion with Employee: (What was the employee's side of the story? What did you tell the employee?)

_____
_____
_____

Date _____
Signature of Supervisor _____

Date _____
Signature of Witness _____

Employee's Comments : _____

_____
_____
_____

Date: _____
Signature of Employee_____

EXHIBIT C

SAMPLE "FIRM BUT FAIR" WARNING LETTER #1

Dear Joe:

Because of the seriousness of the matters we discussed relating to your evaluation, I want to put this in writing so that there will be no misunderstandings later.

Joe, I want you to know that we value the service that you have given us. As I have told you, I strongly feel that you can contribute greatly to the success of our company in the future. We want you to contribute and to be a part of it. However, a number of negative factors have developed that we absolutely must address.

My deep conviction, which I have expressed to you, is that no company can succeed if there is disharmony and lack of cooperation on its staff. Our company is no different than other companies in this regard. These job–related problems that we have discussed simply must be remedied. Specifically, here are some of the areas of our concern:

INSERT DESCRIPTION OF JOB–RELATED AREAS OF CONCERN.

Joe, again I want to make clear that we want you to succeed with us and to be a valued part of our organization. However, I want to also make clear that these problems which we have discussed must be corrected, or we will have no alternative but to terminate your employment. In line with our discussions, you and I will meet again after 30 days to evaluate the situation.

Sincerely,

Joe's Boss

EXHIBIT D

SAMPLE "FIRM BUT FAIR" WARNING LETTER #2

Dear Sally:

So that there is no misunderstanding, we want to put in written form to you our deep concerns about your job performance. We have talked with you on numerous occasions in the past concerning various aspects of your unsatisfactory performance.

Sally, we want you to clearly understand that we have every hope that you will become a satisfactory and valued employee here at our company. We think you have the capacity of doing this. However, your job performance to date has simply been unsatisfactory and we cannot tolerate it further. To do so would be unfair to your fellow employees. In reviewing the background, we note the following:

INSERT JOB–RELATED DETAILS (INCLUDING PAST DISCIPLINE).

Most recently, the following has occurred:

INSERT JOB–RELATED DETAILS.

Again, Sally, we want you to know that we would like nothing more than for your work performance to improve and for you to have a long and fulfilling career with us. However, we will not tolerate this continued unsatisfactory performance. You must clearly understand that if there are repeated instances of such unsatisfactory performance, we will have no alternative but to terminate your employment.

Sincerely,

Sally's Employer

PART II: SAMPLE LETTERS

◆

4

Recruitment and Offer Letters

4-1: Acknowledgment of Receipt of Resume in Response to an Ad

Dear Ms. Banks:

Thank you very much for expressing an interest in the position of director for our *Public Policies Affecting Children* program. At present we are assembling resumes and during October will request interviews with those individuals who seem to combine strong public policy experience with a range of other skills. If we do seek a chance to speak with you in-depth, we will contact you within the next two weeks to determine your interests and availability to meet. Unfortunately, time will not permit us to see everyone who has contacted us.

Virtually every resume is a reminder of the number of committed and talented people interested in improving conditions in our city. We appreciate hearing from you.

Sincerely,

4-2: Acknowledgment of Receipt of an Unsolicited Resume

Dear Mr. Perry:

Thank you for submitting your resume to *Walden Pharmaceuticals* for employment consideration.

An appropriate member of our employment staff will review your correspondence to determine if a suitable opening exists. Should you qualify for a currently open position, we will contact you promptly. If you do not hear from us, a position that matches your qualifications is not available at this time.

We appreciate your interest in our organization and wish you every success in your job search.

Sincerely,

4-3: Acknowledgment of Receipt of Resume from Unqualified Candidate

Dear Ms. Brewster:

I have received and reviewed your letter and resume. At the present time, we do not have an editorial opening and can offer you no future encouragement. Should such a position become available, we would be looking for someone with previous editorial experience and at least an M.A. in art history and/or English. Since your background is not an exact fit to our requirements, I would suggest you contact other area museums. Your qualifications may better match their criteria.

Thank you for your interest in the *Woodstock Institute of Art*, and the best of luck to you.

Sincerely,

4-4: Resume Forwarded to Another Division

Dear Mr. Walters:

Thank you for your recent correspondence regarding employment opportunities in the marketing department of *Templeton Creative Services.*

We have carefully reviewed your background but, unfortunately, have no openings at the present time where the requirements match your special qualifications. It is possible, however, that our advertising department may have a suitable opening, so I have taken the liberty of forwarding your file to them. If there is interest on their part, they will contact you directly.

We appreciate your interest in *Templeton* and wish you success in your employment search.

Sincerely,

4-5: Request to Schedule an Interview

Dear Ms. Kwan:

Thank you for taking the time to discuss career opportunities with our representative at the Women's Career Conference.

As you know, the purpose of our visit is to select qualified individuals to fill entry-level positions in our Management Associate and Sales Associate programs. The hiring needs for our training programs are quite modest; for 1996 we are seeking 50 candidates on a worldwide basis. From your excellent qualifications we believe you may be one of the fifty we are looking for.

4-5: Request to Schedule an Interview (continued)

We will be scheduling in-house interviews at our headquarters in Philadelphia during March. If you are available and still wish to be considered for one of the programs, please contact our offices at (800) 555-xxxx to arrange a meeting.

In addition to this letter, an application and drug consent form are enclosed. Please complete both and bring them with you to the interview. Note that all applicants will be required to take a drug screening test on the same day as their interview.

Your interest in a career with *Carruthers International* is certainly appreciated. We look forward to hearing from you.

Sincerely,

4-6: Post Interview--Company Still Deciding

Dear Ms. Ellwood:

Thank you for your recent visit to *Bristol Engineering*.

While our search is progressing smoothly, its time frame has been longer than anticipated. Please know that we continue to consider you among our active candidates.

A decision regarding the position of engineering manager is expected within two weeks. We will contact you again at that time. If this delay presents a problem, please call us immediately at (800) 772-xxxx.

We appreciate your patience and your continued interest in *Bristol Engineering*.

Sincerely,

4-7: Rejection Without an Interview

Dear Mr. Edwards:

Thank you for submitting your resume to us in response to our recent advertisement for an assistant admissions director here at *Penway University*.

Although we have not yet made a final decision in favor of any one individual, we have now determined that the qualifications of other candidates more appropriately meet our immediate needs. We are sorry to inform you of this, but wanted to let you know as soon as possible.

Your interest in *Penway* is sincerely appreciated. The best of luck to you in your career search.

Best regards,

4-8: Rejection Without an Interview

Dear Ms. Krammer:

Thank you for your recent inquiry advising us of your interest in pursuing a career with *BBD Corporation*.

We have reviewed your resume and samples from your portfolio in light of our current staffing needs and, unfortunately, are unable to offer you further encouragement at this time. This is in no way a reflection upon your fine career development, but rather, is due to our limited and very specific staffing requirements at this time.

Again, we appreciate your interest in *BBD*. We hope you will soon find the challenging and rewarding position you seek.

Sincerely,

4-9: Rejection in Favor of a Better Qualified Candidate

Dear Ms. Barrett:

Thank you very much for submitting your application to the *Wheatley Humanities Council* in response to our position announcement for a program administrator. We appreciate the time you took to apply and assure you that we reviewed your materials carefully. Your credentials, however, did not best meet our particular needs at this time.

We have hired Brittany M. Smythe to serve as our program administrator. Ms. Smythe holds a B.A. in English literature from Brighton College and an M.A. in arts administration from the University of Fine Arts. She is currently a consultant to the McGinnis Foundation and a special projects manager for the higher education consortium. She has experience in all aspects of the grantmaking process, working with a wide variety of community groups, and in organizing public programs. Her strong liberal arts background and her interest in public policy will help *WHC* implement ***Ties***, a long-range program aimed at showing the connection--and relevance--between the humanities and contemporary issues.

Based on such outstanding qualifications, we believe you will agree that Ms. Smythe was the logical choice for this position.

We will keep your resume on file so it may be reviewed again if a more suitable opening becomes available. In the meantime, we wish you every success in your job search.

Sincerely,

4-10: Rejection After an Interview

Dear David:

Thanks again for your interest in career opportunities in the corporate communications department of *Winston & Harrison, Ltd.* We deeply appreciated the time and effort you expended during your recent visit. We were most impressed with your willingness to share your thoughts regarding your success at *Devonshire*.

David, as I indicated during our last conversation, the status of your candidacy is currently on hold. We have found an applicant who better meets our current needs and, in fact, have made a formal offer which from all indications will be accepted.

From a personal standpoint, I want you to know how much I would have enjoyed working with you. I am hopeful that our paths will cross again in the future. Until then, may I extend my very best wishes for your continued success.

Sincerely,

4-11: Rejection After Several Interviews

Dear Pamela:

Thank you again for your continuing interest in *Paxton Laboratories*. We appreciate the time and effort you devoted to learning about career opportunities with our company. It was our pleasure to host you and Steve during your recent visit.

We have now completed the final phase of our recruitment process for the position of Vice President, Sales and Marketing and, as promised, are notifying all candidates. Pam, we were most impressed with your educational credentials and work experience; however, we have decided to offer the position to another candidate whose background includes the management of a much larger sales force.

This decision was not an easy one. It is always distressing when there are two very well-qualified applicants and only one opening. It is regretful that we could not find a place for both of you.

As *Paxton* continues to grow, there will undoubtedly be other positions for which you could be considered. We will be in touch with you to determine your interest whenever such positions become available.

Best wishes for continued success.

Sincerely,

4-12: Offer Letter--Entry-Level Position

Dear William:

I am delighted to offer you the position of management trainee. Your beginning salary will be $1,300 per month paid on a semi-monthly basis.

As we discussed, your position will require some mandatory overtime on an as-needed basis. You will be compensated for overtime hours that you work as statutory requirements provide. Including overtime, your monthly earnings will be approximately $1,650 per month.

The first ninety days of employment are considered an orientation period for all employees. This provides *Enterprise* with a specific time

4-12: Offer Letter--Entry-Level Position (continued)

to evaluate performance. At the end of thirty days or so you should expect to have a meeting with your manager to discuss your progress. A similar review will occur approximately ninety days after the start of your employment.

Training classes will be held throughout the summer. Please contact me at (214) 995-xxxx no later than Friday, March 28, to schedule your classes. Also, if you prefer to live in a specific area, please be prepared to give us that preference when you call. We will make every effort to accommodate your preferences in light of our specific needs.

I look forward to hearing from you soon. Again, welcome to *Enterprise*. We think you have an exciting career before you.

Best regards,

4-13: Offer Letter--Middle-Management Position

Dear Ms. Washington:

On behalf of *Juno Manufacturing,* I am pleased to extend our offer of employment as Group Leader, Quality Assurance. The specifics of the offer are outlined below:

- Starting salary of $45,000 annually.

- Participation in QPC bonus plan.

- Participation in group insurance and leave benefit plans, as detailed in the current employee guidelines handbook and the enclosed brochure on our flexible compensation program.

4-13: Offer Letter--Middle-Management Position (continued)

■ Three weeks paid vacation and 12 company holidays.

This offer is contingent upon your signing all of our employment forms (including the receipt for the employee guidelines handbook) and agreeing to the concept of "employment at will."

This constitutes our entire employment offer to you, and any implied or verbal agreements or promises have no force or effect. This offer letter must be returned, postmarked no later than March 12, or the offer will be cancelled. You may indicate your acceptance by returning the original letter, signed and dated, noting your reporting date of April 9. A copy of this letter is included for your records.

The selection process has been very rigorous, and we are pleased to offer you what we believe is an excellent opportunity. We look forward to your joining the *Juno* team and are confident you will contribute to its continued success.

Sincerely,

4-14: Offer Letter--Executive Position

Dear Ms. Daniels:

I am pleased to extend to you a formal offer of employment. This written offer sets forth the entire agreement between you and *Hunter International*. It supersedes all prior agreements and understandings, whether written or oral.

4-14: Offer Letter--Executive Position (continued)

JOB TITLE: Vice-President, Sales

BASE SALARY: $125,000 per year

BONUS: Eligible in January to participate in the executive
       bonus plan.

VACATION: Three weeks plus an additional two weeks for
       personal business.

IMMEDIATE   Ms. Robin Wright, Executive Vice President,
SUPERVISOR   Sales and Marketing

The following is a list of the contingencies to your offer:

1. All employment forms must be agreed to and signed.
2. You will agree to a pre-employment physical and screening.
3. If, within the first year of service, your performance is considered unsatisfactory, the company will continue your employment for a reasonable period of time from the date you are notified.

If you agree to the terms listed here, please sign in the space below and return the original of this letter no later than 5:00 PM on October 29.

We look forward to receiving your favorable reply.

Sincerely,

4-15: Confirmation Letter--Middle-Management Position

Dear Mr. Herrera:

I am pleased to confirm your acceptance of our offer for the position of Research and Development Manager. You will be in the department of Regulatory Affairs and your immediate supervisor is Dr. Kenneth C. Cavanaugh.

Your initial compensation will be $55,000 per year. Upon satisfactory completion of your first year with the company, you will be eligible to participate in the management bonus plan. The amount of the award will depend on the profit of the business and your own performance. A brochure detailing the plan is enclosed. The bonus guideline for your job class is currently 5% when profit goals are met.

Your official starting date will be October 16. After registering with the receptionist in the lobby, please come to the 9th floor at 9:00 a.m. to complete the administrative process.

Please review the attachments to this letter, complete and sign the appropriate forms and bring them with you on your first day. Note the requirement to bring specific documents which establish your identity and employment eligibility, i.e., a valid driver's license and Social Security card.

If any questions remain, please give me a call. If you are agreement with the terms stated in this letter, please acknowledge by signing where indicated below and returning the duplicate copy of this letter.

Once again, I am confident that the challenge of this position will meet your expectations. I look forward to hearing from you to confirm your start date.

Sincerely,

Orientation and Company Policy Letters

5-1: Information Packet for New Employee

Dear Ms. Harris:

Congratulations on your new position as senior analyst with the *Centauri Group*. We wish you every success in your career with us.

Please find enclosed paperwork that you will need to review prior to your starting date, as well as several enrollment cards and information sheets to complete and return to Human Resources at your earliest convenience:

1. Temporary Entry/ID Card--You will need this card for entry into the building and access to certain secured areas. Please provide the information requested then sign the card where indicated.

2. Federal and State Tax Withholding Forms (W4)--Please complete according to the instructions.

3. Employee Eligibility Verification (Form I-9)--The *Immigration Reform and Control Act of 1986* makes the employer responsible for verifying the identity and employment eligibility of all employees. The law requires employers to request and examine certain documents to confirm employees are who they say they are and that they are eligible to work in the United States. This includes U.S. citizens, permanent residents and nonimmigrant visa holders. If you are unable to provide these documents within three days of your hire date, you must produce a receipt showing you have applied for the proper documents. Otherwise you will be removed from the payroll.

5-1: Information Packet for New Employee (continued)

4. Emergency Notification Sheet--Please provide the names, addresses and phone numbers of at least two individuals who may be contacted in an emergency.

5. Employee Handbook--This manual provides an overview of the company's policies and procedures. It should be studied carefully. Please sign the form on the last page to acknowledge the booklet's receipt.

6. Conflict of Interest Policy--This document outlines employee actions that would be considered detrimental to the company's best interest. Please review the policy then sign the attached certification form. By signing you agree to abide by the rules stated in the policy. Purposely violating these rules could be cause for disciplinary action, up to and including termination.

7. Insurance Program Brochure--This brochure provides a summary of the company's various insurance programs (medical, dental, life, etc.). At the end of it you will find premium information. Please review this information thoroughly before electing your insurance coverage.

8. Health Insurance Information and Enrollment Forms--These sheets compare the many health care options offered by the company. Once you have decided which program will best meet your needs, please complete the appropriate forms.

There is a great deal of information in this packet. Please take your time and go through each document carefully. Should you have any questions about any of the material, don't hesitate to contact me or my assistant. Either of us may be reached at 217-679-xxxx.

Sincerely,

5-2: Training Schedule for New Employee

Dear Justin:

Welcome to *Bankston Associates* and the HR department. We are looking forward to seeing you next Monday. You have a busy week ahead of you, so I hope you will bring all your energy and enthusiasm.

Your first five days will be filled with intensive training. During this time I have tried to keep meetings to a minimum, just in case you should need me. Please don't hesitate to come to me or any other member of the HR staff if you have questions or need help.

As you know, Shawntal Anderson, our current benefits coordinator, will be leaving shortly after your arrival. He has a wealth of information about benefits issues, so spend as much time with him as you can. Before his last day in the office, please be sure to ask for him for his key contacts at our various vendors.

In addition to working with Shawntal every moment possible, here is what you can expect your during your first week:

Monday   9 to 5:   Review new hire orientation process, STD procedures, & open enrollment procedures [especially as related to 401(k) issues]

Tuesday   9 to 11:   Overview of job description procedures

Wednesday   9 to 5:   Job evaluation training

Thursday   9 to 5:   Review life insurance and pension program

Friday   9 to 12:30: LAN and HRIS training

Once again, welcome to *Bankston Associates*. We know you will be a wonderful addition to our staff.

Sincerely,

5-3: Change in Hiring Policy

To: All Employees

Fr: Human Resources Manager

Re: New Hiring Policy

For many years the corporation has had a policy for all of its operations that prohibits the hiring of relatives into the same company. While there are many valid reasons for this policy, it has kept some qualified individuals from applying for positions with us.

The current unemployment rate is low and all companies in the state, ours included, are having trouble filling their openings. Due to these extraordinary circumstances, the corporation has allowed us to temporarily suspend the limitation on hiring relatives until the end of next year. The temporary policy guiding this new practice will read:

HIRING OF RELATIVES: People who are related by blood or by marriage may be employed by the Company based on their qualifications for the job, provided these guidelines are followed:

* No relative reports directly to another relative.
* No relatives work in the same department.

Management reserves the right to apply this policy even more strictly based upon the position the relatives would hold in the company, their exact relationship, and other pertinent circumstances which may affect the best interest of the Company.

We hope this change will enable all of you to make more referrals of good people you believe will be an asset to us. If you have any questions about this policy, please speak with your supervisor or someone in the HR department.

5-4: Incentive for Employee Referral

To: All Employees

Fr: Human Resources Manager

Re: Employee Referrals

As most of you know, we have been growing so rapidly we are now short staffed. We have been trying, with little success, to hire a number of new people into the company. Unfortunately, other companies in our area are trying to do the same thing. All of us are having a difficult time finding enough qualified people to fill these new openings.

One of the best ways of finding good people is through referrals from current employees. We have greatly appreciated your referrals in the past and would like to encourage even more of them in the near future. As an incentive, every employee who makes a referral that results in a successful hire will now receive something in return for the effort.

Effective immediately, we are implementing a new reward system for people who refer job candidates. If someone you refer is actually hired and successfully completes 90 days on the job, the company will give you a $75 "thank you." Here's how it works.

When you refer a person for a job, complete a referral form and give it to HR. This form will be attached to the person's job application. Note that the form must be submitted prior to the person's interview. If two or more people refer the same individual for a job, the first referral received by HR will be eligible for the incentive.

Since the person must work for 90 days before you can receive your bonus, be selective in the type of people you refer. Make sure they are reliable, motivated, etc. It would also be in your best interest, once they are hired, to help them succeed in their new job. With your help they will work out, the company will have a great new employee and you will have $75 in your pocket. Everyone wins!

5-5: Bonus for Employee Referral

Dear Ken:

Several months ago you referred Angela Cortez for the entry-level position of merchandising assistant. You certainly are a fine judge of character. Of the 15 applicants for the job, Angela seemed to have the most promise. She had a strong academic background and a genuine interest in the company as a whole, not just the department where she might be working.

Angela has just completed her first six months on the job. Her manager is very pleased with her progress to date.

Our company's continued growth and success depends on finding the best people for each position within the organization. Without your help we may never have found Angela. Please accept the enclosed check for $150 as a "finder's fee" with our thanks and gratitude.

If you know anyone else like Angela, send them our way. We may have just the place for them.

Best regards,

5-6: Change in Smoking Policy

To: All Employees

Fr: Human Resources

Re: New Smoking Policy

For years the medical community has warned smokers of the hazards of smoking. Until recently the general attitude in society--and within most companies--was that if someone still wished to smoke in spite of the risks, that was his or her choice.

There is now overwhelming evidence that smoking is not only harmful to those with the habit, it is equally dangerous to the non-smokers around them. New studies confirm that secondhand smoke can adversely affect the well-being of individuals who have never taken a puff of a cigarette, cigar or pipe.

In the interest of improving the health of all employees, the company has decided to adopt a new policy that will prohibit smoking anywhere within the building. The no-smoking policy will become effective in three months. In the interim, those who smoke will only be allowed to do so in private offices or outside the building. Smoking in common areas, such as washrooms and cafeteria, is banned as of today.

The company realizes that even with all its negatives, smoking is still a difficult habit to break. To help those who are ready to try, the company will be sponsoring smoking cessation classes beginning next week. The classes are free. Anyone who would like to attend should contact the employee relations manager at ext. 307 to register. Additional information about the program and the specific dates and times of the meetings will be sent to you.

We know the next three months will not be easy, but we believe that in the end we will all benefit from our new smoke-free environment.

5-7: Casual Days

To: All Employees

Fr: Chief Operating Officer

Re: Casual Days

You asked for it and now you have it. Beginning this Friday, every Friday will be a casual day.

Though we encourage you to express your personal taste and style, remember that you or your co-workers may have visitors in the office on Fridays. We need to ensure that our workplace reflects a professional and positive business environment at all times. Please keep this in mind when selecting your attire for the office on Fridays.

In accordance with our new casual day policy, a task force of employees developed the following casual business attire guidelines which all employees must follow. Casual business attire does not include:

- faded jeans and/or denim-type clothing
- shorts
- halters (or other bare shoulder outfits)
- bare legs or feet
- gym shoes
- lycra-based clothing (e.g., leggings)

Neat jeans may be appropriate, provided they are in good condition and are not extremely faded.

If you have any questions, please discuss them with your manager or a member of your Human Resources team.

5-8: Casual Days

To: All Office Employees

Fr: Human Resources Manager

Re: Dress Code

Up to now those who work in the office have been required to follow a professional dress code. Only formal business wear was considered appropriate, particularly for those who interact with our customers. Recently, however, you have brought to our attention the need to change our standards regarding office attire. As was pointed out, in some work places certain times of the year or certain days of the week are designated as "fashionable casual."

After a thorough discussion of this topic and a review of common practices in our industry, the management team has decided to broaden the dress code for office staff. Effective immediately, each Friday will officially be a "casual day." Tasteful casual clothing will be acceptable wear on Fridays. This includes casual slacks, nice jeans, etc.

We encourage those of you who wish to dress casually on Fridays to do so, but in a way that will still be respectful to our customers. Worn out jeans, sweats, and shorts would generally be outside the definition of casual and not acceptable attire on any day of the week.

We hope this will be a positive change for everyone and will make our company an even more inviting and comfortable place to work!

5-9: Harassment Policy

To: All Managers

Fr: Human Resources Director

Re: Professional Environment

The company believes it is the right of all its employees to perform their jobs in an environment free from personal harassment. Harassment of any nature and in any form (verbal, physical or visual) is strictly against company policy and will result in disciplinary action.

As a manager, you are expected to maintain the highest ethical standards in carrying out your responsibilities. Further, you are accountable for any misconduct of a sexual, racial or ethnic nature made by your staff. Sexual harassment--whether by innuendo, physical conduct or verbal suggestiveness--and derogatory ethnic or racial remarks are all unacceptable. Managers are expected to take immediate corrective action when they learn of such occurrences.

It is extremely important to investigate all complaints and allegations, and to encourage staff members to feel comfortable about reporting any incidents of harassment. Let staff members know that they can discuss these incidents with you in confidence. You should then report the suspected abuses to your superior and the human resources director. The same procedure should be followed if you are the one who observes the harassment. Confidentiality will be maintained to the greatest extent possible.

A copy of the company's newly revised harassment policy is attached. If you have any questions regarding the new policy or the procedures that should be followed to investigate and resolve incidents of harassment, please feel free to contact me at ext. 2189.

5-10: Sexual Harassment--Preliminary Investigation

PERSONAL AND CONFIDENTIAL

Dear Ms. Edwards:

We recently received a complaint that you may have violated *Ivy Communications*'s sexual harassment policy. Sexual harassment includes unwelcome sexual advances, requests for sexual favors and other verbal, visual or physical conduct of a sexual nature. Employees who violate this policy are subject to disciplinary action up to and including termination.

All allegations of sexual harassment are investigated immediately, as outlined in the attached copy of the company's sexual harassment policy. Any individual who may have knowledge of the alleged incidents and events described in the complaint against you will be interviewed to gather facts. You and the person who filed the complaint will also be interviewed.

It is imperative that this matter remain confidential. Please help us by not discussing the complaint or the investigation with anyone other than myself. You should not be retaliated against because a complaint has been filed, nor should you retaliate against the person you suspect brought the complaint. If you do feel you are being retaliated against, please notify me immediately.

I will contact you within the next few days to let you know when your interview is scheduled. If you have any questions or I can be of assistance, please feel free to contact me at ext. 325.

Sincerely,

5-11: Sexual Harassment--Results of Investigation

PERSONAL AND CONFIDENTIAL

To: Paul Lane

Fr: Human Resources Manager

Re: Outcome of Sexual Harassment Investigation

Grace Fremont and I recently completed our investigation of Tamara Cahill's allegations of sexual harassment against Jonathan Fowler. Mr. Fowler openly admits he "swatted at her (Tamara Cahill) and hit her buttock." Based on our review and subsequent discussion with you, we recommend Mr. Fowler receive no less than a five-day suspension without pay.

You indicate that Mr. Fowler is a "good," long-term employee and that he has a tendency to touch others during the course of conversation. Regardless of his intentions in this situation, Mr. Fowler must be made aware that actions of this nature will not be tolerated.

Additionally, Mr. Fowler must be advised that he is not to behave in any manner that may be perceived as retaliation. Ms. Cahill must be assured that she will be free from harm and that appropriate action has/will be taken against Mr. Fowler.

If you have any questions regarding the recommendation or would like further details regarding the investigation, please call.

5-12: Call-In Pay Policy

To: All Managers and Supervisors

Fr: Human Resources

Re: Call-in Pay for Non-Exempt Staff

Occasionally, non-exempt employees are asked to come in to work at times other than their scheduled work hours to help with emergencies. The time they are here may be short (often as little as 15 minutes), but the inconvenience of being called away from home and travelling to the plant is great. Regular pay for the brief time they are here usually amounts to little and may not even pay for the gas it took them to get to and from work.

At other times, non-exempt employees may come in to work at their regularly scheduled time, but due to power outages, machine problems, etc., they are unable to do their jobs and are sent home for the day.

To be fair to employees in such situations, the company has implemented a call-in pay policy. This new policy is effective immediately.

If non-exempt employees are called in to work beyond their regular work hours, or if they come in for their normal shift but can't work due to mechanical or electric failure, a minimum of two hours will be paid to the employees regardless of how long they are clocked in. This means that any time worked up to two hours would merit two hours pay. Once an employee has worked two hours, he/she would be paid only for the actual number of hours worked.

The intent of this policy is not to give "bonus pay" for being called to work. It is to ensure that when employees are called in, they are paid enough to at least make the trip worth their time.

5-12: Call-In Pay Policy (continued)

When an employee is entitled to call-in pay, the supervisor will mark the timecard to alert payroll so the employee will be properly compensated. It is the supervisor's responsibility to monitor this new practice and to ensure that call-in pay is given whenever appropriate.

If you have any questions regarding the policy or its administration, please call HR at ext. 489.

5-13: Violation of Absenteeism Policy

Dear Mr. Darcy:

Reliability is a quality *Boston Steelworks* looks for in all its employees. It is especially important for one in your position. Production schedules cannot be maintained if associates do not report to work or contact their managers of their intent.

Your recent actions show that your dependability is questionable at best. You have not come to work for the last four days nor have you tried to reach your supervisor to explain the reason for your absence.

Unexcused absences over a period of three or more consecutive days are considered a voluntary resignation. In accordance with the company's policy, your employment has been terminated as of Thursday, January 25. Please contact the Human Resources department to arrange an exit interview, at which time you will be required to return all company property.

Should you have any questions, you may contact me at (617) 968-xxxx, ext. 545.

Sincerely,

5-14: Warning for Violation of Security Policy

Dear Ms. Moore:

This letter will serve to recap our meeting of March 15. This meeting was held to discuss your violation of company rules #4 (failure to observe security regulations) and #20 (permitting others to use company identification badges).

On Sunday, March 6, at approximately 9 PM you invited a relative into the Computer Center through an outside door. This entrance was under the control of your department and was to be watched as if it were maintained by the security department. Allowing a non-employee to enter a "controlled" area without clearance or a visitor's badge is a violation of company security and department procedures.

At roughly 10:30 PM the same day a security guard observed your relative in the center wearing your badge. Permitting others to wear your company identification badge is a violation of our rules of conduct.

Since you were the senior person on this shift, you had an additional degree of responsibility in security matters. Your decision to disregard company and departmental security policy is a matter of extreme concern to us. This notice of caution is being sent to you to stress the seriousness of your offense. In addition to the notice, you will be suspended for one day without pay effective March 17.

The safety of employees is not a matter to be taken lightly. Should you violate the security policy again within the next year, you will be subject to further disciplinary action, up to and including termination.

Sincerely,

5-15: Warning for Excessive Tardiness

Dear Ms. Sutton:

Cranston Incorporated cannot effectively meet customers' needs when its employees are habitually late or do not show up at all. Every now and then a late arrival will be unavoidable, but this should be the exception, not the rule.

Nearly every day for the last two weeks you have arrived at the office at least 20 minutes after your scheduled starting time. Your manager has spoken to you about your tardiness and though you assured him the problem would be corrected, it has not. The matter has now been referred to the human resources department for resolution.

Chronic tardiness is unacceptable and will not be tolerated. The next time you arrive after your starting time, you will be docked as outlined in the company's attendance policy. A copy of the policy is attached for your review. If the tardiness continues, it will be cause for further disciplinary action.

Up until two weeks ago you seemed to have no trouble arriving at the office punctually. If your recent lateness has been caused by some change in your circumstances that you would like to discuss, I would be happy to speak with you. If the issues are of a more personal nature, you might feel more comfortable talking to someone outside of the office. In that case, I would urge you to contact the EAP.

I sincerely hope you will rectify this problem immediately. If I can help in any way, please let me know.

Sincerely,

5-16:   Warning for Violation of Dress Code

Dear Mr. Tyler:

For the third time in the last six weeks, you have come to work in a manner that clearly violates *American First Federal's* dress code:

■ In mid-July, you arrived for work in frayed jeans and a workshirt.

■ In early August, you showed up wearing a short-sleeved shirt, safari shorts, a baseball cap and sandals.

■ Yesterday, after being on vacation for three weeks, you returned with the beginnings of an unkempt beard.

On each occasion Mr Washington, your manager, made it clear that your attire was unacceptable then gave you an assignment away from the public for the rest of the day. After yesterday's incident, Mr. Washington asked the HR department to assist him in the resolution of this problem.

Mr. Tyler, in all three cases you have violated the bank's policy on dress and personal appearance. No employee, male or female, is allowed to wear casual clothing to work. Male employees are not permitted to wear beards. In your position you have a great deal of public contact and your appearance sends messages, whether favorable or unfavorable, to our clientele. Beards and worn jeans are simply not in keeping with the bank's conservative image.

Effective immediately, you must come to work in attire that adheres to the guidelines noted in the attached policy. Further, before being allowed to return to work, you must shave your beard. If you refuse, you will be suspended without pay until you comply with our requests.

We hope this matter will be quickly resolved. Please call if you have any questions about the policy or the issues raised in this letter.

Sincerely,

5-17: Violation of Attendance Policy

Dear Mr. Brewer:

As we discussed last week, your attendance since you began working at *Jensen Clothiers* has been far from acceptable. In less than six months you have had a total of five unexcused absences. According to company policy, this number of absences could be grounds for termination. In your position, attendance is especially important since many people depend on your work to get their jobs done. When you are absent, it creates a number of problems throughout the company.

According to your manager, you have shown a great deal of expertise in the accounts payable position. She wants you to stay and believes you could be quite successful. For this reason, we are giving you one last chance to prove your reliability. If you wish to remain employed with *Jensen,* your attendance must improve ***immediately***. For the next three months you will be expected to arrive for work every day and on time. If you are absent or tardy within this three-month period, further disciplinary action will be taken, up to and including immediate termination.

Your manager values the contribution you make to your department and does not want to lose you. You have been given the opportunity to improve your attendance record, a very important aspect of your overall performance. Please use this "second chance" wisely.

Sincerely,

===

I have read this warning and understand it. I have also received a copy for my records.

_____   _____
Signature   Date

5-18: Warning for Abuse of Company Phone System

Dear Mr. Blake:

This notice of caution is being issued in response to your violation of company rule #8, excessive use of the company phone system for non-business calls.

Since December 1994, you have been abusing your phone privileges by making an average of 100 calls per month, not including toll-free numbers. Specifically, between September and November you made 341 calls, 176 of which were off-net toll calls. Sixty-five of these were made in a single day, November 21. This represents one call every 7 minutes that day.

Your justification for these calls was that you were calling and hanging up before any significant cost could be charged. The calls were to adult book stores, striptease clubs, phone sex numbers and escort services. The calls were intended to harass the owners of these businesses.

This form of "recreation" on the job is not an appropriate use of company time. Abuse of the company phone system must be stopped. Your productivity has suffered as a result of this activity and that will be reflected in your annual performance review. In addition, we are referring you to our employee assistance program for help with your concern about these particular business interests.

This purpose of this notice of caution is to communicate to you the seriousness of this offense. A second offense within 12 months of this date will result in possible termination.

Sincerely,

5-19: Warning for Unprofessional Conduct

Dear Marsha:

We are in receipt of a copy of a memo that you distributed last Friday. In this memo you insulted and berated many of our company's best clients. We consider the memo, and your actions in preparing and distributing it, to be extremely unprofessional and unacceptable.

This is a public relations firm and, as switchboard operator and receptionist, you are the first person who has contact with the public. Your role is an important one and the impression you make may mean the difference between our gaining or losing customers. Consequently, your unprofessional behavior is of considerable concern.

This letter is to notify you that your employment with the company will only continue under these conditions:

1. You show immediate improvement in the handling of your duties and in all of your actions while serving as a representative of the company;

2. You are helpful and courteous to all callers and visitors, even when they may treat you in a less than cordial fashion (to assure this, your calls and your conduct in the reception area will be monitored at random);

3. You no longer criticize or otherwise refer to any callers or visitors in a derogatory fashion, regardless of the circumstances.

We have counselled and warned you in the past about similar instances of unprofessionalism, and yet you have not made any effort to improve your conduct. This is your final chance to correct your behavior. The violation of any of the conditions noted above will result in your immediate discharge.

Sincerely,

Compensation and Benefits Letters

6-1: Summary of Benefits for New Employee

Dear Ms. Kennedy:

Congratulations on your new position as creative director with *Aberdeen Advertising*. We are pleased to have such an accomplished professional joining our staff.

During the interviewing process you and your new manager probably had many discussions concerning salary. Benefits, however, may have been covered only briefly. This letter will highlight the benefits to which your are now entitled as an *Aberdeen* employee.

If after reviewing the letter you would like further details about any of the benefit programs, please don't hesitate to contact the benefits and employee relations manager at 207-995-xxxx.

GROUP INSURANCE BENEFITS:

1. Hospitalization/Medical/Dental

   - Provided free for you and your eligible dependents.
   - Begins on the first of month following your start date.

2. Life Insurance/Accidental Death

   - $100,000 basic life insurance and $100,000 accidental death insurance provided for you at no cost.
   - An additional $100,000 in coverage available for purchase by you at the cost of 24 cents per $1,000 per month.

6-1: Summary of Benefits for New Employee (continued)

PENSION/RETIREMENT SAVINGS PLANS:

5. Pension Plan

   - You will be eligible after 1 year of employment.
   - When eligible, you will pay 1% of base salary up to Social Security base and 2% of salary above Social Security base.
   - Your benefit upon retirement will be 1.75% times final average salary, times years of service, minus 1/2 Social Security award.

6. Retirement Savings Plan (401K)

   - You will be eligible after 1 year of employment.
   - When eligible, you may contribute up to 6% of base salary and defer federal taxes.
   - The company matches the first 5% at 100%

SICK PAY/LONG-TERM DISABILITY

7. Sick Pay and Long-Term Disability Coverage

   - You may receive 2 months' full salary for personal illness.
   - After 2 months off the job, an additional 4 months pay at 65% of base salary is provided.
   - After 6 months off the job, 60% of salary will be provided as long as you are disabled, up to a maximum of $4,000 per month, in coordination with Social Security

MISCELLANEOUS

8. Relocation Expenses

   - Cost of transporting household goods paid in full by the company.
   - Real estate commission to sell your home paid by the company.

6-2: Employment Issues

To: All Employees

Fr: Human Resources

Re: Human Resource Studies

In the last few weeks you have probably been hearing a lot about several important human resources projects now in progress. During this time the HR department has been working closely with a consulting firm to study a number of issues that impact all of us. The purpose of this memo is to briefly describe each project, what it is to accomplish and its present status.

1. *Revision and updating of job descriptions*--All employees were asked to complete a job survey form describing their jobs. This information will be used to develop more specific job descriptions that are consistent with the *Americans With Disabilities Act* requirements. Having more specific job descriptions should help expedite performance appraisals.

2. *Refinement of performance review process and form*--The consulting firm will recommend a new review process and form by the end of the quarter. Both the form and review procedure were developed based on interviews with managers, union stewards, and a random sample of employees along with the result of surveys completed jointly by HR and the consulting firm. Training will be provided to all managers and employees once the process and form have been adopted.

3. *Review of salary structure*--As you know, there are fewer levels of management than there were three years ago. We now want to take a hard look at our salary structure to make sure it fits the current organization. We would also like to recognize top performers. The consultants will be making several recommendations to help us achieve these objectives.

6-2: Employment Issues (continued)

4. ***Investigation of the expanded use of incentives*--**For the coming months and years, the company has set several aggressive goals. Incentives are an effective way to motivate team performance toward these goals. Managers, union stewards and a random selection of employees have identified several situations where the use of incentives may be appropriate. We will be prioritizing these situations within the next month. We will then be able to identify some parameters within which a specially created incentive design team could work. All incentive options will have to be consistent with existing company rules and policies and will have to be communicated with the bargaining unit.

5. ***Finalizing a personal development plan*--**The company cares about the personal development of all its employees. Personal development in an employee's current job can prepare him or her for other jobs within the organization, should other positions become available. In the coming weeks the staff training and development manager will be coordinating a formal personal development program. This program has been developed in conjunction with our consultants based on feedback from a number of employees at various levels within the organization.

To make these projects a success we would like your input to ensure we are all working to achieve the mission and goals of the organization. We do not know if salaries will change as a result of this work. Our objective is to have recommendations in by May 15 for review by the board of directors. If you have any questions or suggestions, please call the employee relations manager at ext. 207.

6-3: Compensation Incentives

To: All Employees

Fr: Human Resources

Re: Innovation in Total Compensation

A "Gap Analysis" was recently conducted by Maggie Spencer, one of our HR consultants. She interviewed management, staff and union representatives to identify areas within the following categories that may be appropriately addressed by an incentive team:

Key Success Factors--

- Customer service
- Financial results
- Empowered teams
- Quality
- Productivity
- Corporate culture (communi-cation, creativity & innovation)

An incentive team has been formed and is currently brainstorming to design a plan that provides the opportunity for all employees to share in the financial gains resulting from improvements made from their involvement. Team members include: Barbara Jones, Mark Ryan, Robert Chang, Kim McClennan, Peter Burns, Jeremy Phillips, Mary Prescott, William Bell, Marguerite Torres, and Emma Wright. Ms. Spencer will serve as the team's facilitator.

The team's major responsibilities will be to:

1. Design a plan that is consistent with the employee involvement process, strategic objectives, accounting systems, communication practices, market conditions and existing improvement opportunities.

2. Make design decisions through consensus decision-making and popular vote.

6-3: Compensation Incentives (continued)

3. Develop an effective communication process that keeps all employees informed of the plan development.

4. Present the proposed incentive program to the Executive Committee and representatives of the union.

5. Once approved by senior management and the union, present the final program to all employees.

The final approved program will be organization-wide and will cover all employees. It will be team-based and in effect for one year. However, the incentive will not be added to base pay.   At the end of the one-year trial period, the program will be reassessed.

6-4: Employment Issues: Follow-up

To: All Employees

Fr: President and CEO

Re: Status of Human Resource Studies

Over the last several months we have made a great deal of headway on our various human resources projects. The purpose of this memo is to inform you of the progress of each program.

1. ***Revision and updating of job descriptions***--Revised job descriptions have been prepared based on your input. Managers will review them one last time before the descriptions are approved. Once finalized, all employees will receive a copy of their newly approved job description.

6-4: Employment Issues: Follow-up (continued)

2. *Performance review process and form*--The executive team reviewed and decided upon final recommendations from the consulting firm for our new performance review system. Following is a summary of the new performance review process and form:

- The primary goal of the performance review is to facilitate feedback between managers and employees.

- Performance expectations (behavioral and results-oriented) will be set at the beginning of each review period.

- There will be ongoing communication between employees and managers about performance as well as ongoing training.

- Personal development will be tied into performance review and each employee will be given feedback on individual performance expectations.

- There will only be three ratings for each performance expectation (exceeded, met or did not meet). There will no longer be an overall performance rating on the form.

- There will be a common annual review date for teams. Depending on the team to which you belong, you will be reviewed on one of these four dates: 10/15, 1/15, 4/15 or 7/15.

3. *Review of salary structure*--Interviews have been conducted with managers, union stewards and a random sample of employees and their views about our current pay structure were gathered. Additionally, market pricing data have been collected. We want to be sure our salaries are competitive with others in our industry. Our consultants will be analyzing this information and making recommendations about the pay structure in the next two months. It is not known if salaries will change as a result of this work.

6-4: Employment Issues: Follow-up (continued)

4. *Use of incentives*--Information on the use of incentives was gathered at the same time information was collected on the salary structure. The outcome of these interviews was discussed in detail in a recent memo about the "Gap Analysis" conducted and the team that has been formed as a result of that study to develop the pay incentives.

5. *Personal development plans*--The executive team adopted formal personal and career development programs at its last meeting. These programs were designed in your interest and with your input. In the coming weeks, you will be hearing much more about these two special programs.

As always, we would like to hear from you if you have any thoughts, comments, suggestions or questions concerning the programs. Feel free to contact the employee relations manager at ext. 207.

6-5: Leave of Absence

Dear Brenda:

Your request for a leave of absence from the university has been approved effective October 21. Before taking the leave, however, you must use all your vacation. You may either take the time off or request a lump sum payment for all days you have earned..

During a leave of absence some privileges are safeguarded, while others are not. In your case your seniority will be protected for the purposes of benefit accrual, but you will not earn benefits while on leave. Your present position cannot be held for you; should you wish to be considered for future openings, you will have to submit a new employment application.

6-5: Leave of Absence (continued)

Enclosed with this letter is a record of employment for unemployment insurance purposes. It certifies that your job was insured and gives the address of the payroll department, which has the necessary records to verify your earnings. This form hasn't been sent to encourage you to apply for unemployment insurance or even to suggest you would qualify. In the event you should decide to apply for unemployment benefits, fill the form out completely and take it with you to the unemployment insurance office.

Brenda, we appreciate your many contributions to the university during your five years with us. Should you have any questions concerning your leave, please give me a call or drop by.

All the best to you in your future enterprises.

Sincerely

6-6: Leave of Absence--Continuation of Medical Coverage

Dear Julie:

It is my understanding that your unpaid leave of absence will begin on September 1 and end October 31. During this time you may continue your medical coverage or allow it to lapse. Should you choose to keep your health benefits while you are away, you will be responsible for the full amount of the premiums.

Your cost will be $250.75, payable the last day of each month while you are on leave. Your first payment will be due September 30. If it is not received by that date, your coverage will be terminated. Should coverage lapse, you will have to wait the standard period of three

6-6: Leave of Absence--Continuation of Medical Coverage (continued)

months when you return to active employment before you are again eligible for health insurance benefits.

Please make your checks payable to *Yardley Press* and mail them to my attention at: 1 Waverly Plaza; Merrill Springs, TX 75123.

If you have any questions, or if the circumstances regarding your leave status should change, please give me a call at (214) 345-xxxx.

Sincerely,

6-7: Health Plans--Response to Employee Suggestions

Dear Mr. Franklin:

Thank you for your comments regarding the company health insurance plans offered at your location for the 1995 plan year.

The Anderson Group would like to satisfy each employee's request for benefits. Frankly, that is the motivation behind offering three different plans at each location. Each plan has a budgeted amount of premium dollars to operate within and the plan design fits into a budget. The health care plans take into account any suggestions of an advisory group of employees. The benefits are designed to fully meet the needs of as many employees as possible. If we offered the same benefits in each plan, there would not be a need for more than one plan. Most employees appreciate the choice of different health care options.

Your suggestions will definitely be considered and weighed when we begin evaluating the plans for 1996. Possibly, we could increase the

6-7: Health Plans--Response to Suggestions (continued)

deductible in Health Wise or reduce hospitalization to give us the premium needed to cover preventative benefits.

If you or any other employee has additional suggestions about the health plans, please submit them before September 1995. This is when the decisions concerning the plans takes place.

Once again, thank you for sending in your suggestions. The company always appreciates feedback from its staff.

Sincerely,

6-8: Request for Short-Term Disability

Dear Richard:

We have received your letter asking to be placed on short-term disability (STD). We were very sorry to hear about your accident during your recent skiing trip to Steam Boat Springs.

Before your request can be considered, the three forms enclosed must be completed:

1. Short-Term Disability Application
2. Authorization to Use Compensated Time
3. Termination of Disability Leave

A brief description of each document and an explanation of the STD approval process follows:

6-8: Request for Short-Term Disability (continued)

■ **Short-Term Disability Application**

Short-term disability cannot be granted until it has been formally requested.   Completing the STD application is the first step in this process. The application has three sections, each to be completed by a different party:

• Section one should be filled out by you, the requestor, then signed where indicated.

• Section two is for your physician to complete. It is recommended that you hand deliver the application to your physician then follow up with him or her to ensure that the necessary information has been provided.

• Section three will be completed by Human Resources.

The application, with the first two sections completed, should be returned to my attention within ten days of your receipt of the form.

Once your application is returned, it will be evaluated and approval will either be granted or denied. If your application is approved, your recovery will be monitored throughout the Short-Term Disability period by a medical consulting firm. They will confer with your physician and review your records to determine the status of your condition. Please be sure to let your physician know someone from the consulting firm will be contacting him. If you physician does not discuss your case with the firm's representative, your benefits will be delayed.

■ **Authorization to Use Compensated Time**

This form authorizes payroll to apply any available compensated time to your timesheet while your STD application is being reviewed.

To receive a paycheck during this time, you will be required to use all your sick days. Once your available sick time has been exhausted, you

6-8: Request for Short-Term Disability (continued)

may authorize use of any personal and/or vacation time you have remaining. Any personal or vacation time used *after* the initial ten-day waiting period will be reinstated once an approval is made. Personal and/or vacation time used *during* the initial waiting period will not be reinstated.

■   **Termination of Disability Leave Form**

This form indicates when you are able to return to work and should be completed at the end of your disability period. Your physician will complete the top half and you should complete the bottom half. It is important that you bring this form with you the day you return to work.

I am available if you need additional information or simply have questions regarding the forms or the STD procedure. You may reach me at 315-745-xxxx.

Sincerely,

6-9: Family and Medical Leave Act

To: All Employees

Fr: Human Resources

Re: Company Policy on Family and Medical Leave Act

Bixby Enterprises will comply with all applicable provisions of the federal Family and Medical Leave Act (FMLA). This Act applies to all *Bixby* employees with at least one year of service and who have worked a minimum of 1,250 hours during the year before the leave is requested.

6-9:   Family and Medical Leave Act (continued)

Employees who qualify are entitled to up to a combined total of 12 weeks of unpaid leave per calendar year for:

1. the birth of a child or caring for the newborn;
2. the placement of a child for adoption or foster care;
3. caring for seriously ill family members (spouse, child or parent);
4. the employees own serous health condition which prohibits him/her from doing his job.

If a leave is desired for reasons other than those listed above, a regular leave of absence should be requested.

"Serious health condition" is defined as an illness, injury or impairment that requires either hospitalization or continuing treatment by a health care provider. For employees, it is a condition which prevents job performance. For a child or parent, for example, it is an illness which prohibits a child from attending school, or prevents an adult from attending to normal activities.

An FMLA only applies to situations which require absences of more than one week. Short-term illnesses from which a person can be expected to recover quickly and easily are not included. For example, if an employee is ill for three days, this would not count as part of the FMLA they may be entitled to during the year. However, if he/she were ill for several weeks, this would apply toward their FMLA.

When an employee needs to take an FMLA leave for a serious health condition, he/she must obtain a certification form that is available in the HR department. This form must then be completed by the employee and the health care provider. The provider must certify the need for the leave and its probable duration. When a leave is foreseeable, the certification form must be completed and returned to the HR department 30 days in advance. As much notice as possible should be given if the need for leave arises unexpectedly.

6-9: Family and Medical Leave Act (continued)

Unless prior approval is obtained from the General Manager, employees will be required to use all paid leave, if available, before taking unpaid leave. The paid leave will be counted as part of the FMLA leave. If, for example, an employee is entitled to 5 sick days (one week), he would only receive 11 weeks of unpaid sick leave. Similarly, an employee entitled to 5 sick days (one week) and 10 vacation days (two weeks) is eligible for 9 weeks of unpaid leave. Note than an employee cannot use paid sick leave to care for a sick family member.

While on FMLA leave, employees must submit a status report to the company every 30 days. The report should be sent to the employee's manager and indicate progress and intent to return to work. When the employee does come back from leave, a release form must be provided.

When eligible employees are granted FMLA leave, and they comply with all requirements under the Act and the company policy, they will be guaranteed their original job or an equivalent position when they return. No loss in status will occur from taking an approved FMLA leave. However, if an employee fails to return as agreed, loss of his position (including termination) may occur.

The only exception to this guarantee of status and position upon return from leave applies to certain highly compensated employees. The top 10% of salaried employees may be denied this guarantee if "reserving" their position would cause substantial and grievous economic injury to the operations of the company. Notification that reinstatement may be denied must be given to such employees at the time the leave is requested.

During unpaid FMLA leave, no additional benefits such as sick leave or vacation time are accrued. However, as long as the employee pays his share of the cost of insurance plans, all medical and dental benefits will continue.

6-10: Employee Assistance Program

Date: January 5, 19xx

To: All Employees and Their Families

Fr: Human Resources

Re: New Benefit--Employee Assistance Program

The Association is pleased to announce its new Employee Assistance Program. This service is now offered as a practical and helpful resource for all full-time employees and their dependent family members. At some point in their lives all people are faced with problems that seem overwhelming and insurmountable. Left unresolved, these problems can adversely affect day-to-day living, personal and professional relationships and work performance.

The Employee Assistance Program will be administered by United Counseling Services, an acknowledged leader in the field of mental health. The agency has a staff of 300 mental health professionals who are experienced in handling a broad spectrum of personal problems, including alcohol and substance abuse, marital difficulties, depression, grief after a significant loss, financial stress, and child/elder issues.

The EAP is provided as an added employee benefit. Telephone consultations are available 24 hours a day and are free of charge. There are no charges for up to six counseling sessions per calendar year. If referral for additional counseling or other assistance is needed, the EAP counselor will recommend the best service at the most reasonable cost. The employee will be responsible for any services beyond the scope of the EAP; however, in many cases, medical benefits will cover a portion of the expenses.

6-10: Employee Assistance Program (continued)

Participation in the EAP is voluntary. Employees may seek help from the program on their own or at the recommendation of a manager or co-worker.   Under no circumstances will referral occur without the employee's consent.

Privacy is essential to anyone who decides to seek counseling. All conversation with the EAP counselor is confidential. No one will know what was discussed unless you choose to tell them.

In the next few weeks, orientation sessions will be scheduled to familiarize all employees with this program. Representatives from the consulting firm will be available to answer any questions you may have.

Many difficult problems can be resolved when competent, professional and confidential assistance is accepted an early stage. The Employee Assistance Program is designed to put employees directly in touch with the help they need. The decision to request or accept this help is yours.

Should the need arise, we urge you to take advantage of this new service. If you would like further information or wish to use the EAP before the orientation session, please call United Counseling Service at 1-800-234-HOPE.

6-11: Addition to Benefits--Smoking Cessation

Date: April 9, 19xx

To: All Employees

Fr: Human Resources

Re: New Eligible Health Expense--Nicotine Patch

We heard you! In response to your requests, and as part of our commitment to healthier lifestyles, *J.B. Manufacturing* is pleased to announce that the cost of the transdermal nicotine patch has been approved as an eligible expense within the company's medical plans.

Proof of the completion of an approved smoking cessation course is required before any part of the cost for the patch can be reimbursed.

The expense for the patch is subject to deductibles and copayments. You can be reimbursed up to $170 per treatment, with a lifetime limitation of two courses of treatment not to exceed $350. The cost of the smoking cessation program is also subject to deductibles and copayments. Although there is no dollar limitation on these programs, you are restricted to those courses that have been approved by the company (see the attached list).

If you or your eligible dependents wish to take advantage of this enhancement, you should do the following:

1. See your doctor and obtain a prescription.
2. Purchase the patch and keep the receipt.
3. Enroll in, and complete, an approved smoking cessation program.
4. Obtain a certificate or diploma showing you have completed the program, as well as a receipt for the cost of the program.
5. Submit a claim form, your receipts and your certificate to our insurer.

If you have any questions regarding this new benefit, please contact the benefits manager at ext. 578.

6-12: Child Care Benefits

To: All Employees

Fr: Chief Operating Officer

Re: New Child Care Assistance Benefits

Many employees have expressed an interest in the company offering some form of child care assistance to employees. Our research is complete and we are pleased to announce that in 1995 we will offer two new benefits to help you balance your family and work life:

- an on-site child care center; and
- discounts to child care centers near our office.

ON-SITE CHILD CARE CENTER

Over a year ago, we joined forces with other companies in our building to form The Child Care Consortium. The Consortium explored several child care options including:

- opening an on-site child care center;
- negotiating discount rates at neighborhood child care centers;
- providing discount vouchers to all eligible employees;
- purchasing slots at neighborhood child care centers; and
- offering dependent care flexible spending accounts;

As with other members of the Consortium, we feel it is worth the financial investment to open an on-site child care center on the first floor of our building. An agency with expertise in setting up child care centers across the country has already begun the planning of the new Center which is expected to open in January.

We will have 25 of the 100 slots at the Center. Children ages six weeks to five years are eligible for enrollment. Since the company will subsidize a portion of the child care cost, employees will receive a discount

6-12: Child Care Benefits (continued)

at the Center. Enrollment will be on a first-come first-served basis.

Over the next few months, look for more details regarding the opening of the Center, hours of operations and the rate schedule.

DISCOUNTS AT LOCAL CHILD CARE CENTERS

We recognize that the 25 slots in the on-site child care center will fill quickly, so we wanted to offer another option to employees who can't get in the on-site center or who prefer another child care center. We've negotiated special rates for our employees at the following child care facilities:

- Rainbow Day Care Center;
- ABC Tots;
- Lindview Children's Center;
- June's Day Care; and
- Wee World.

The discounts range from five to 15 percent off the regular weekly child care cost. In order to receive the discount, you must show your employee identification card each week when you pay your tuition.

This discount program will begin in January and remain in effect until the Centers and/or we decide to cancel it. Centers can only take a certain number of children in each age group, so some facilities may not have openings to meet your needs. Please call the Center to find out if they have an opening. Your Human Resources representatives have brochures describing each Center and our negotiated rate.

We hope these new benefits will be of value to you. If they make it easier for you to meet your family and work demands, they will have met our objectives.

If you have any questions concerning either benefit, please call your Human Resources representative.

6-13: Summary of Benefits to Terminated Employee

Dear Alexa:

This letter will review the benefits to which you are entitled as a terminated employee of *Resurrection Mental Health Associates*. Your eligibility for the benefits was determined based on your date of hire (August 6, 1984) and the date of your separation from the company (October 21, 1995).   A brief description of each benefit follows:

VACATION: At the time of your departure from the company, you had 7 unused days and 13 additional days accrued. You will be compensated for these 20 days of earned vacation..

SEVERANCE: Because your position was eliminated, you are entitled to two weeks of severance for each full year of service as outlined in *Resurrection's* severance policy. You will, therefore, receive 22 weeks of compensation. This will be paid to you in a lump sum once you have signed and returned the severance agreement given to you on October 27.

DISCRETIONARY BONUS: Company policy states that any employee of who leaves the company prior to the end of the year is ineligible for a discretionary bonus. Given the circumstances of your departure, however, the Company has decided to compensate you for all objectives met from January through October.

LIFE INSURANCE: You may apply for an individual life insurance policy within thirty-one (31) days after the termination of your group life insurance. An application for conversion coverage is enclosed for your completion.

PENSION: You are fully vested in *Resurrection's* pension plan and are entitled to receive pension benefits beginning on the last day of the month following the month you turn 55. Please keep the organization

6-13: Summary of Benefits to Terminated Employee (continued)

apprised of your whereabouts so your future pension payments may be processed in a timely manner.

401K PLAN: The necessary forms to authorize a distribution from your 401K account are enclosed. Please complete the sections highlighted on the Request for Distribution form. To receive your account balance, you must also complete the enclosed addendum. Before filling out these forms, you may wish to speak with a tax professional.

HEALTH INSURANCE: You are eligible to continue your health insurance under the Consolidated Omnibus Budget Reconciliation Act (COBRA) of 1985, or you have the right to obtain conversion coverage without providing proof of good health.

If you decide to enroll in COBRA, you have 60 days from the date your *Resurrection* coverage ends to inform *Resurrection* of your intention to continue or discontinue coverage. Information concerning this program is enclosed in this packet. You should contact me as soon as possible to let me know if you wish to continue in the health insurance program.

If you would prefer conversion coverage instead, you must apply in writing and pay the first premium to our insurance carrier within thirty-one (31) days after your group coverage ends. The thirty-one (31) days starts on the date your coverage actually ceases even if your are still eligible for benefits because you are totally disabled. A conversion form is enclosed should you select this option.

Should you have any questions regarding any of the benefits, don't hesitate to contact me. I may be reached at (513) 925-xxxx.

Sincerely,

6-14: Eligibility for Retirement Plans--Current Employee

Dear Ms. Whitfield:

We are pleased to inform you that effective January 1, you will be eligible to participate in the company's pension and retirement savings plans. A brochure which briefly highlights the two programs is enclosed. Should you wish more detailed information, please see your employee handbook.

If you wish to enroll in the programs, please complete the attached enrollment forms. The completed forms along with a document verifying your date of birth (as outlined on the reverse side of the pension form) should be returned in the envelope provided no later than December 10.

Participation in the programs is not mandatory. If you decide not to enroll at this time, simply complete the applicable refusal cards and return them by December 10.

Decisions regarding retirement are very important and should be given serious thought.   We believe these two programs are among the most important in our benefit package. They offer each employee the chance to make his or her future more secure.

If you have any questions after reviewing the materials, please give me a call at 612-409-xxxx. I would be happy to speak with you.

Sincerely,

6-15: Eligibility for Pension Benefits--Retired Employee

Dear Ms. Chen:

At the time of your retirement from *Dickerson Law Resources* you were not yet entitled to any pension benefits. As of March 1, you will become eligible to receive benefits in accordance with the company's pension plan. The accompanying retirement benefits summary sheet shows your pension amounts. The details of these benefits are outlined in the enclosed materials.

You may begin receiving pension benefits as early as the date indicated in the section titled "Early Pension Options," or you may choose to begin payments on the first day of any month following this date. In the latter case, benefits will be higher than the early pension amount, but less than the full benefit for which you become eligible at age 62. If you elect to defer your pension, it will be your responsibility to notify the company at least three months prior to the date you wish your pension to begin.

Once you have made a decision on your pension option, please complete and send back the appropriate forms. If you elect the early pension option, please return:

♦ the "Election Form for Immediate Pension Options";
♦ the "Withholding Certificate for Pension or Annuity Payments";
♦ a copy of your birth certificate (or other proof of age);
♦ the direct deposit form, if this method of payment is chosen.

If you elect to defer the start of your pension until a later date, please return:

♦ the "Election Form for Deferred Pension Options";
♦ the "Survivor Income Beneficiary Designation form indicating your marital status and your election or waiver of survivor income during the deferral period.

6-15: Eligibility for Pension Benefits--Retired Employee (continued)

If we have not heard from you within 90 days from the date of this letter, we will assume you have decided to defer your pension benefit to age 62. If applicable, your pension will be reduced for survivor income coverage calculated from your date of retirement to the date your pension begins.

Once payments begin, you may not select another option.

To ensure the accuracy of our records, please keep us informed of any change of address. If you have any questions or require any clarification, please give me a call at (218) 715-xxxx.

Sincerely,

6-16: Open Enrollment

Date: November 9, 19xx

To: All Employees

Fr: Human Resources

Re: Open Enrollment Period

It's time for our annual benefits open enrollment period. Enclosed is information for you to review to help you make your election decisions for the medical, dental, FSA and the 401(k) programs. Human Resources representatives will be available every Tuesday and Thursday during the open enrollment period to answer any questions you may have regarding the programs. Completed enrollment forms for all programs should be submitted to your HR representative no later than **Friday, December 2.**

6-16: Open Enrollment (continued)

ACTIONS REQUESTED

■ Medical and dental coverage -- Complete an enrollment form only if you wish to make changes to your medical or dental coverage. Be sure your form is completely filled out, including your signature and the Social Security numbers for all eligible dependents. Enrollment forms are enclosed for your use.

During open enrollment you can:
► transfer from your current medical and/or dental plan to another;
► change from single to family coverage or vice versa; and/or
► add eligible dependents not previously enrolled.

■ Flexible Spending Accounts (FSA) -- Each year, a new enrollment form must be completed by employees interested in participating in the program, even if you are currently enrolled in the program. Enrollment forms are available from your Human Resources representative.

During open enrollment you can:
► increase or decrease payroll deductions; or
► begin enrollment.

■ 401(k) -- Complete an enrollment form if you want to make changes. An enrollment form must be completed for newly-eligible employees even if you do not wish to contribute. You do not need to complete a form if you do not want to make any changes.

During open enrollment you can:
► increase or decrease the amount deducted from your paycheck (i.e., your deferral amount/percentage);
► re-start payroll deductions; or
► suspend payroll deductions.

Once you change your deferral amount/percentage, you cannot change it again until the next open enrollment period.

6-17: Pension Benefit--Lump Sum Payment

Dear Mr. Powell:

The *Glen Oaks Savings and Loan* pension plan provides a lump sum payment in lieu of monthly payments if, at retirement, the lump sum equivalent of the pension is less than $3,500. Since the actuarial equivalent of your pension is $3,257.19, you will be receive a one-time lump sum payment in accordance with the plan's provisions. This distribution represents the total value of your benefit entitlement.

As of January 1, 1993, lump sum distributions from qualified pension plans are subject to a mandatory 20% withholding of federal income tax unless the *entire* distribution is rolled over into an IRA or other tax deferred plan. An important notice is enclosed concerning the tax treatment of lump sum distributions. Please read it carefully and consult a tax specialist before making a final decision regarding the treatment of your distribution.

If you choose to take payment of your distribution directly, return:

1. the signed copy of this letter;
2. the W4-p form should you wish additional taxes withheld above the mandatory 20%.

If you elect the rollover option, please return:

1. the signed copy of this letter;
2. Attachment A indicating your choice of institution to which 100% of your distribution should be sent.

Regardless of the option you select, we will need a copy of a document that shows proof of your age.

If you have any questions concerning the distribution, how it was calculated, etc., please contact me at (314) 852-xxxx.

Sincerely,

6-18: Pension Benefit--Vested Terminated Employee

Dear Janice:

As a vested terminated employee of *Artemis International Travel, Inc.*, you are entitled to pension benefits. The attached summary sheet shows the dollar amount of your retirement benefits under the company's pension plan. There are a number of options you should consider carefully before making your final elections on how to receive your distribution. The decisions you make about your retirement income will affect the rest of your life. Given the great impact your choice will have on your present and future finances, we strongly urge you to seek advice from both legal and tax specialists.

The following materials are enclosed to help you decide how and when you wish to receive your benefit:

- An overview of options available under the pension plan;
- A brochure which discusses major issues to consider regarding your benefit;
- Details of your pension benefit election;
- Tax information.

After you have studied the materials, you will need to decide how you would like your benefit paid. Prior to making any election, however, you will have to provide:

1. An original or certified copy of your birth certificate or other document that shows proof of your age. If you plan to select a joint and survivor form of payment, you will also need to submit proof of your spouse's or joint annuitant's age. These documents will be returned to you after our review.

2. Your completed election form, including:

- Any necessary spousal consent (if you are married and elect

6-18: Pension Benefit--Vested Terminated Employee (continued)

a form of payment that reduces the otherwise automatic survivor payments to be made to your spouse).

■   Your elections regarding tax withholding.

Since the value of your pension benefit is less than $10,000, you may elect to receive your benefit now in the form of a lump sum payment, or you may defer your benefit until the age (as early as 55) you choose to retire. Whatever your choice, you must complete the enclosed pension benefit election form and return it within the next 60 days.

If you choose a monthly benefit to begin at a later date, you can always change your election provided the change is made before the monthly benefit starts. Once your benefit begins, your election cannot be changed.

If you are at least 55 and wish to start your benefit now, please let us know. It will take a few months from the date of your retirement (or the date you return your completed election form after termination of employment) until you receive any payments. However, your payments will be retroactive to the date your benefit was scheduled to begin.

Please be sure to let us know of any changes in your address and/or phone number. If you have any questions or need further information regarding your pension benefit, do not hesitate to call. I may be reached at (415) 666-xxxx.

Sincerely,

6-19: Insurance Benefits--Retired Employee

Dear Ms. Hollister:

Enclosed is your retiree benefits booklet, "Partners in Your Healthcare and Life Insurance Benefits." It contains information regarding the medical, dental, and life insurance plans available to *Omni Media Services* retirees. It also includes the current year's rate information.

If you wish to enroll in any or all of the plans, please complete the retiree insurance election form and the beneficiary designation form. Both forms should be returned to our offices within 21 days following the termination.

All insurance benefits (medical, dental and life) will be administered by the Retiree Medical Administration at company headquarters. After your benefits become effective, please direct any questions or requests for claim forms to Juanita Sneed, the retiree benefits manager, at:

Omni Media Services, Inc.
Retiree Medical Administration--QBC 24
5 Glenolden Plaza
Ghiradelli, CT   05213
1-800-303-xxxx

The Ghiradelli office is open Monday through Friday from 8:30 AM to 5:30 PM, Eastern Standard time.

If you have any regarding the enrollment procedure or the booklet, feel free to contact me at (219) 432-xxxx.

Sincerely,

6-20: Survivor Benefit

Dear Mrs. Harper:

We are sorry to hear of your husband's death and extend our sincere sympathy.

At this time we would like to advise you of the survivor income benefit to which you are entitled under the terms of the *McClain Company*'s pension plan. As your husband's survivor, you are eligible to receive an annual benefit of $930.24, payable for your lifetime in monthly amounts of $77.52. Your first check comes to $185.04 and covers the period from December 20 through February 28. It will be mailed to you during the last week of January.

Please complete the enclosed federal withholding tax form (W4-P). If you wish your checks deposited into your bank account, also fill out the attached direct deposit form. As I mentioned when we spoke, there will be a one-month waiting period before the checks will be deposited automatically. A return envelope has been enclosed for your convenience.

In order to complete our files, we will need a copy of your husband's death certificate as well as a copy of a proof of age document for you (birth certificate, driver's license, etc.).

Once again, Mrs. Harper, let me extend our condolences. If you have any questions, don't hesitate to contact me at (123) 456-xxxx.

Sincerely,

6-21: Change in Paycheck Distribution

Date: February 2, 19xx

To: All Employees

Fr: Human Resources Manager

Re: Paycheck Distribution

With all the confusion of different shifts and schedules, it has become increasingly difficult to distribute paychecks on a day when everyone is working. If you look throughout the company, you can now find someone with a workweek that ends almost any day of the week. Unfortunately, our payroll system cannot reflect this variability in working schedules. Consequently we have had to limit the timeframe during which checks will be distributed.

Paychecks for the night shift will be printed and ready for distribution by 5 PM Thursday afternoon. Only those people working Thursday night will receive their checks that evening. ALL day shift employees, and any night shift employees not working Thursday night, will receive checks on Friday. To repeat, no checks will be distributed Thursday except to night shift employees who are here working that night.

What this means for now is that if you are not scheduled to work on Friday, you must come in and pick up your paycheck. Checks for all employees not working that Friday will be kept in the HR office and distributed from 8 AM to 5 PM on Friday. We promise that someone will be here to hand out checks during all of those nine hours. Just a reminder: if you send someone else to pick up your check (even your spouse), we must have an authorization from you.

We realize this procedure is difficult for a number of people. We are not doing this because we don't want to pass out checks early, be responsive to your needs, etc. We honestly are unable to produce the checks consistently before Thursday night with our current payroll system. We are working on the purchase and implementation of a newer system that would allow us to process payroll faster, but in the meantime, we must follow the procedure outlined above.

Training and Career Development Letters

7-1: Personal and Career Development

To: All Employees

Fr: CEO

Re: Company Commitment to Personal and Career Development

The purpose of this memo is to tell you more about our new Personal and Career Development programs. Our organization believes personal development is important and benefits both the individual and the company. Developing personally to improve performance is everyone's responsibility if we are to remain competitive. Career development, or planning for future jobs, is an option for every employee.

PERSONAL DEVELOPMENT PROGRAM

Purpose: To ensure that all employees gain and maintain the skills and knowledge to meet the needs of the organization.

Objectives: To assure that:

1. Personal development needs, development activities and a timeframe for those activities are identified for every employee;

2. Those development needs and activities identified as priorities are incorporated into future performance expectations;

3. The organization identifies and offers high quality, creative and economical developmental activities and communicates these activities to managers and employees.

7-1: Career Development (continued)

Role of Staff and Training Development Manager: Acts as development resource and advises management and teams about creative and cost-effective development approaches to meet program objectives.

CAREER DEVELOPMENT PROGRAM

Purpose: To offer employees the opportunity to explore career options within the organization, both horizontally and vertically, to ensure open positions are filled by valued internal candidates.

Objectives: To assure that:

1. Employees are formally given the opportunity to discuss career options, either with their manager or human resources;

2. Information about open positions is available to all employees;

3. Managers, at their discretion, and/or the staff training and development manager, can help the employee identify a career development plan to prepare for future positions should the need exist.

Role of Staff and Training Development Manager: Acts as career counselor and, as requested, assists employees and managers in understanding career options and position requirements within the organization.

You will learn more about these two programs at the upcoming performance review training. If you have any questions before then, please contact the Human Resources department at ext. 538.

7-2: Training and Development

To: All Managers

Fr: Human Resources

Re: Training and Development

Staff training and development is a crucial component of the Company's commitment to promotion and mobility from within. It is also an integral part of the management process. Training should be seen as a continuous process that varies with individual needs. The object is either to improve performance in the current job or to prepare for a particular job or promotion. Your staff's training needs should be addressed continually, not just during the formal performance evaluation.

Your role as a manager is to coach and counsel your staff throughout the year to help them better their performance on the job. You should also ascertain what their individual goals and ambitions are for the future and give them guidance as to realistic expectations for promotions and/or transfers. A two-way discussion of the development needs of each staff member should be part of the annual performance review.

If you are considering a job change or promotion for someone on your staff, be sure that he or she has been adequately prepared for the new role. Training can be appropriate, and is sometimes essential, for even the most talented and motivated employees.

Often training can be readily provided through on-the-job advice, extra supervision, or the counsel of other managers or colleagues. Assigning staff members to temporary positions, either within the department or in other areas of the Company, can also serve as a form of training. If you and the employee feel that outside expertise and resources would be helpful, you can consult with the human resources director for any current training programs that may be available and appropriate.

7-3: Educational Assistance Program

To: All Employees

Fr: Human Resources

Re: Educational Assistance Program

To encourage continued education to help you better perform the responsibilities of your job, the company has developed an educational assistance program. This program reimburses expenses and fees for workshops, seminars, and college courses that are job related. Book fees are not covered. The conditions and criteria for participation in the program are outlined below:

Criteria

1. All regular full-time employees who have completed six months of service with the company are eligible for this benefit.

2. The course(s) you wish to take must be job related.

3. The course must be approved in advance by your manager, the division director and the HR manager.

How to Apply

1. Complete an education reimbursement application.

2. Give the completed form to your manager at least two weeks before the start of the course. A course outline and verification of the cost must accompany the reimbursement application.

7-3: Educational Assistance Program (continued)

Reimbursement

1. Fees/tuition are reimbursed 100% for grades of A and B and at 75% for a grade of C or "pass."

2. Receipts for the fees/tuition must be submitted with the final grade or completion certificate along with a course evaluation form signed by your manager. All items should be forwarded to HR.

3. You must continue to be a regular full-time employee during the complete length of the course in order to be reimbursed.

Required Courses and Workshops

If you are required to attend a seminar or other course of study by your manager, either on your time or the company's, any expenses will be covered under the company's training and development budgets. The submission of a reimbursement form is not necessary.

If you have any questions or would like more details regarding the program, or would like an application form, please contact Human Resources.

7-4: Review for Promotion--Academic Setting

Dear Ms. Willoughby:

This is to advise you that your appointment as assistant circulation librarian in the *Contra Coastal University* library expires on November 1. According to the terms of your appointment, you are now eligible for review for promotion to associate circulation librarian.

7-4: Review for Promotion--Academic Setting (continued)

Assistant librarians are expected to advance in rank to the associate level within three years, although a one-year extension is granted under special circumstances. Individuals not promoted within that time will not be reappointed to the staff. Staff are allowed only one opportunity to be reviewed for promotion. Promotion recommendations are made by the university's Academic Promotion Review Board.

Criteria for promotion to associate circulation librarian include:

1. Outstanding performance as an assistant librarian or the equivalent rank/position at another institution, successful completion of assigned responsibilities and evidence of initiative beyond basic assignments.

2. In addition to outstanding job performance, evidence of excellence as an assistant librarian may include, but not be limited to, the following characteristics and achievements:

♦ The ability to act independently and creatively to enhance the library's effectiveness;

♦ Significant contributions to the operation of a specific library unit in the form of suggestions, plans and actions;

♦ Effective relationships with patrons and staff members at all levels;

♦ Evidence of growth in librarianship, archival work and/or relevant subject areas;

♦ Effective participation in library task forces, committees, etc.

♦ Publications or presentations in librarianship or related disciplines. In consideration of publications or other presentations, content and form as well as quantity will be taken into account.

7-4: Review for Promotion--Academic Setting (continued)

To assist the Review Board in its evaluation, please submit the following documents/information to human resources no later than September 15:

1. A cover letter summarizing your accomplishments and highlighting those you feel are most important. This may also include future plans and goals.

2. A complete and up-to-date curriculum vitae including educational history, professional and academic honors, organizational memberships and offices held, institutional and community service, publications and other professional contributions.

3. Names, addresses and phone numbers of at least three individuals who are in a position to comment specifically on your performance and qualifications with a brief explanation of why you selected each one. At least one source should be a member of the academic staff here at the university.

4. Any material documenting evidence of professional growth as mentioned, but not limited to the examples given.

May I take this opportunity to wish you success in your review. If at any time during the review process you have questions concerning procedures, please feel free to contact me.

Sincerely,

7-5: Request for Reference--Academic Setting

Dear Mr. Thompson:

Ms. Sarah Willoughby has been a member of the staff of the *Contra Coastal University* library for the last three years. She is now a candidate for promotion from the position of assistant circulation librarian to associate circulation librarian. Sarah feels you are one of the persons in a position to comment knowledgeably upon her professional qualifications and achievements. We are asking you for your written evaluation of her performance based on, but not restricted to, the criteria specified in the enclosed materials.

Among the most important characteristics of each candidate is the ability to make decisions then to carry out those decisions effectively. Quality of judgement is difficult to evaluate or define, but it is critical to the performance of academic responsibilities. Flexibility of intellect and action are important considerations as well. We would like you to predict or describe the performance of this candidate in the event of a change of assignment or in the context of a changing environment, even though no new assignment may be involved.

We would appreciate a specific indication of whether or not you would recommend Ms. Willoughby for promotion and the basis on which you are making your recommendation. Your comments will be kept in the strictest confidence, so please be candid. Please return your response, marked confidential, to my attention no later than October 10.

Sincerely,

7-6: Notification of Promotion--Academic Setting

Dear Ms. Willoughby:

I am pleased to inform you that you have been recommended for promotion to the rank of associate circulation librarian in the *Contra Coastal University* library. The recommendation has been accepted and will be transmitted to the Provost by the start of the next fiscal year.

Please accept my congratulations and those of your colleagues on your performance since joining the staff. Only by retaining talented and highly motivated academic staff members can this library system hope to maintain its distinction. We shall continue to rely on you in this effort.

If you have any questions regarding your new position, please give me a call at your convenience. I may be reached at ext. 574.

Sincerely,

7-7: Thank You for Evaluation--Academic Setting

Dear Mr. Thompson:

Thank you for taking the time to respond to our request for your comments on Sarah Willoughby. I am happy to report that the review was positive and Ms. Willoughby will be promoted to the rank of associate circulation librarian

Your evaluation played an important role in the committee's decision, and we are grateful for your help.

Sincerely,

7-8: Apprenticeship Appointment--Skilled Trades

Dear Robert:

It gives me great pleasure to inform you that you have been accepted in the 1997 Skilled Trades Apprenticeship Program. Your appointment is effective March 28. Your classroom activities will begin March 30 at 10 AM at the Mariner's Institute.

As you requested, you have been given an apprenticeship position in the inside machinist department. Your transfer will be effective on Monday, April 7. You should contact the superintendent to schedule your start time and work assignments.

Within the next week or two, I will be contacting you to schedule an orientation interview. At that time you will also need to complete some paperwork required by the state.

Robert, you can be justifiably proud of your selection to this prestigious program. Based on the comments of those who have recommended you, I am confident you will work hard and successfully complete it. *Poseidon Shipping* is looking forward to your return as a future skilled craftsperson. In this new capacity, we know you will make an outstanding contribution to the company.

Again, congratulations. If you have any immediate questions, please feel free to contact me at ext. 902.

Sincerely,

7-9: Request To Promote Employee

Eric Bailey has been performing the job of heat transfer operator for a number of years now. For approximately the last four years, he has been given responsibility for the entire heat treat process and its people. The heat treat process has grown in complexity and the quality standards it must meet are higher. It has also added several additional people during the past year, and has basically become its own department. Because of these changes, and the functions Eric is required to perform, I believe that this position should rightfully be redefined as heat treat leadperson. This memo is to propose that we make this change in the position and promote Eric to leadperson effective January 1.

Below is a list of the job functions performed by the leads in other departments and a statement on each regarding Eric's performance of those functions.

Essential Functions of a Leadperson

1. *Works with little to no daily supervision, making the day-to-day decisions for the entire department.* Eric runs the heat treat process with almost no supervision. He has full responsibility for it, and is often called in on all shifts to address problems.

2. *Completes all paperwork for the department, including time cards, production paperwork, etc.* Eric handles all paperwork associated with heat treat and its employees, including totaling time cards, completing production records, keying information into the computer, and maintaining control charts. He also handles all miscounts for the department.

3. *Performs quality inspections on the product during and after the process.* Eric does all the inspections for temper in the department. He voluntarily started the control charts used in the department, and is involved in ongoing quality improvement teams. He interacts regularly with QC and engineering regarding quality issues.

7-9: Request To Promote Employee (continued)

4. *Provides training, coaching, and daily supervision to the people in the department.* Eric completes the lead section of the performance review for the people in heat treat. He is involved in interviewing applicants and he trains all new employees in the department. He oversees all people in heat treat, including those on second shift.

5. *Schedules daily work for the department and coordinates work load and materials.* Eric does all scheduling for heat treat and is active at updating production control information on the computer. He designates what the department will work on each day, with little or no input from his supervisor. He runs the forklift and moves material for the department.

6. *Coordinates work with other departments.* Eric completes maintenance work orders, interacts daily with production control, and communicates frequently with all other departments.

7. *Participates in committees, problem-solving teams, etc.* Eric has been very active on a number of committees, including the employee relations committee, safety committee, and a number of problem-solving committees. He provides leadership among his peers throughout the plant, not just in his department.

I believe Eric is currently performing all the duties of a leadperson, and that he should now receive the title and pay to fairly reward him for his outstanding performance. As the company continues to grow, we will need someone formally designated as lead over this area. Also the heat treat function continues to have a major impact on the quality of the product.

Eric's technical understanding of the process makes him a person I can rely on to run that operation almost independently and to stay focused on the quality of the product. I highly recommend we promote Eric as of January 1 and recognize his excellent performance with a raise effective the same day.

8

Restructuring, Downsizing and Layoff Letters

8-1: Announcement of Change in Work Week

To: All Employees

Fr: CEO

Re: Change to Seven-Day Work Week

As most of you know by now, we are planning to begin a seven-day work week with ten working hours scheduled for each of the two shifts. The change will go into effect on January 15.

Why are we doing this? It is without question a significant change for some of the people in manufacturing, especially those in fabrication, packing and the warehouse. There are quite a few compelling reasons. This memo is to outline those reasons for you. In addition, we will also hold meetings with each department next week to discuss the matter further. Please read this memo prior to your department meeting.

Reasons for the Change

Space: We have experienced a tremendous growth in sales volume in 1994 compared to 1993 and expect to see a comparable increase in 1995. As a result, space for production has become a pressing issue much sooner than expected.

Overtime: Along with the crunch on space in 1994, we worked an extraordinary amount of overtime in all departments to meet the increasing pace of incoming orders. Overall, plant-wide YTD overtime through November was 1.8 times what it was through the end of November 1993. Many employees had to work six- and seven-day

8-1: Change in Work Week (continued)

weeks much of the year. Needless to say, many people spent more time at work than at home and had little leisure time.

Capacity: It is clear that the amount of business in 1995 will continue to increase markedly. The unbalanced work flow, the excessive amount of overtime in 1994 and the lack of space make change a necessity.

Options Considered

There are a number of things we can do and have done to make more space available in the plant. We have already moved some operations to the warehouse. Also, earlier in the year we started a second shift in the packing area. This has had a major positive impact on the congestion in the packing department.

Moving the manufacturing operation to a larger building was another option we have considered and it is still a future option. The downside would be business disruptions that would effect several departments. The major problem now is that there are no existing buildings large enough for our operations. We could build our own, but that would be quite expensive. It would also be one to two years before the space limitations would be addressed and we can't wait that long.

Another option is to keep working overtime. Our experience this year has shown, though, that excessive overtime negatively impacts the employee's safety, productivity and personal life. For these reasons, additional overtime was not considered a long-term option.

Reducing our volume was a possible, but questionable, option. Even if we chose not to grow, our funding for improvements and future expansion would be jeopardized. The mid- to long-term consequences of this action could put the future of the company at risk.

A seven-day work week was the one option that appeared to make sense both for the company and the employees. It will eliminate the need for people to constantly work overtime, while increasing our ability to produce more product. It will also level out the flow of work and the space needed to accommodate it.

Who Will be Affected

If a seven-day work week is the most workable solution, the next question was whether all departments needed to move to this schedule. After a bit of analysis, it became obvious that the front end of the plant (extrusion, anodic, and buff & hammer) cannot operate seven days and have fabrication and packing work only five days. The work would pile up, further aggravating the problem of space limitations, and increasing the need for overtime.

Reactions to the Change

During the many months the change to a seven-day week was considered, we requested input from people throughout the company. We asked for their ideas and suggestions. Most employees have expressed approval and see the benefit of the new schedule. They will now have more time with their families since they will have three days off each week.

Obviously some people have reacted negatively to the change and this is to be expected. In time we hope everyone will adapt to the new schedule and find it workable, perhaps even positive.

I would like everyone to know the decision to go to a seven-day work week did not happen overnight. We explored different alternatives for nearly a year. I and the rest of the management team truly believe this is the best solution for the company and the majority of the employees.

If you have any questions or suggestions regarding the seven-day schedule, please bring them to your department meeting next week. I encourage you to come that meeting prepared to openly express your views, and to listen the information that will be presented.

8-2: Announcement of Company Downsizing

To: All Employees

Fr: Vice President and General Manager

Re: Reduction in Force (RIF)

The government has called for further reductions in the cost of our program. This reduction calls for an additional 7% reduction over and above the 15% reduction previously announced. The following actions are required for us to meet this goal:

- The workforce must be reduced by approximately 100 employees effective February 15. This downsizing will address the reduction connected with the budget shortfall from the planned 5% reduction target that we did not achieve at year end. The reductions will primarily affect the program office and engineering. Production operations will not be affected at this time, however, there may be some adjustments necessary in operating supporting organizations.

- Each organization will continue to be expected to reduce its personnel by 5% through normal attrition during the fiscal year.

- A program to reduce all controllable overhead non-personnel budget accounts by 10% in each organization will be implemented immediately. Finance will take the action to revise our current budgets beginning February 1.

It is possible that further reductions will occur later this fiscal year or next year depending on the customer requirements. We will advise you of further developments as we become aware of them.

A RIF is very difficult for all of us, yet it is necessary to adjust our spending levels to meet funding requirements and to keep us competitive for current and future business opportunities. These reductions will be accomplished in accordance with company policies, including provisions covering allowance and outplacement services.

8-3: Announcement of Layoffs

To: All Employees

Fr: Vice President and General Manager

Re: Contract Termination

On January 31, we received official notice from the government that our contract had been terminated. The loss of this contract will mean the immediate elimination of several hundred positions.

Since receipt of the termination notice, we have carefully assessed the existing workload, the impact on the employment levels, and projected workload. Based on this evaluation, we have concluded that we must reduce our workforce by 300 employees in order to remain competitive.

Management has started identifying jobs that might be cut. In addition, the company will offer all employees the opportunity to volunteer for the reduction in workforce. Volunteers, however, must submit their requests to human resources by February 10. Management will then review all requests, but reserves the right to disapprove the voluntary resignation of individuals whose positions are considered key to the successful continuation of the company's operations.

Employees, including volunteers, whose jobs will be eliminated will be notified on February 18. All employees will be eligible for separation benefits, including outplacement services, severance, health benefits, etc.

I have considered all feasible options in light of the contract termination notice. The only realistic decision is to proceed with a reduction in workforce. The Human Resources staff will be prepared to assist those individuals whose positions have been eliminated as a result.

8-4:   Approval to Eliminate Position--Academic Setting

Dear Gia:

Your request to eliminate the position of administrative assistant currently held by Amanda Drake is approved. This approval is based on the following understandings:

- Ms. Drake will receive a minimum of 30 calendar days advance written notice prior to the date of the layoff, not including accrued vacation time.

- No vacant positions currently exist in the department for which Ms. Drake is qualified.

- If the position is reinstated or a comparable one is created within one year from the date of the layoff, Ms. Drake must be offered that position.

- No positions are available to which Ms. Drake can be reassigned within the budgetary unit in accordance with the University's policy.

I encourage you to arrange an interview for Ms. Drake with the staffing specialist so she may obtain assistance in locating continued university employment.

Upon receipt of a copy of the written notification of layoff to Ms. Drake I will send her a letter describing the benefits available to her as a laid off employee.

Sincerely,

8-5: Notification of Layoff--Academic Setting

Dear Ms. Drake:

I am sorry to inform you that your position as administrative assistant in the Physics Department is scheduled to terminate within the next six weeks. You will be placed on University layoff status effective November 22. Official University layoff status may extend for a period of up to one year from your last day worked.

The office of Human Resources will provide you with a letter describing the benefits, training and educational opportunities, and other assistance available to you. We would also be happy to help you find another position within the University to help you avoid, if at all possible, any period of unemployment or break in service. I encourage you to check the University's weekly employment newsletter and to contact the staffing specialist for information regarding positions available on campus for which you may qualify.

Enclosed along with this letter is a record of employment for unemployment insurance purposes. It serves to certify that your job was insured and shows the correct address at which payroll records are kept. The intent of mailing this form is not to encourage you to apply for unemployment insurance (it may not be applicable in your situation), or even to suggest that you would be qualified to receive benefits. However, should you decide to apply for benefits, you must bring this completed form with you to the unemployment office.

The best of luck to you. If you have any questions, please feel free to contact me.

Sincerely,

8-6: Notification of Impending Layoffs

To: All Employees

Fr: Human Resources

Re: Company Merger

Our company's merger with *Delta Advertising* will be finalized within the next few weeks. The joining of the two companies will result in a stronger organization with an expanded client base and competitive advantages that neither company could achieve alone. Along with the benefits of the merger, however, there is also a downside.

During the negotiations key staff studied the service functions of both companies Not surprisingly, it was learned that many functions were duplicated. To reduce the overlap, the management has suggested the consolidation of certain functions as well as the restructuring of selected departments. Though every effort will be made to retain as many positions as possible, it is inevitable that some jobs will be eliminated.

A special separation package will be available to all employees who may lose their jobs as the result of the merger. The package is being announced now in order to clarify what would occur in the event of job displacement. Following is a summary of the enhanced benefits for regular full-time employees. These benefits will only be provided if the employees work until the end of their assignments and complete any required documentation prior to leaving.

SEVERANCE BENEFITS:

Severance benefits will be calculated on current base salary at the time of termination. All employees affected will be given a 60-day notice of termination date plus enhanced benefits based on their years of service:

8-6: Notification of Impending Layoffs (continued)

Service Completed	Enhanced Severance
1 to 4 Years	4 months
5 to 7 Years	6 months
8 to 11 Years	8 months
12 to 15 Years	10 months
16 to 19 Years	12 months
20 to 20+ Years	15 months

OTHER SEVERANCE BENEFITS:

Vacation: Any unused annual vacation and personal days will be paid.

Pension Enhancement: For employees whose age and service equal 70 as of end of year termination, a special one-time pension enhancement adding three years to age and three years to service will be applied to their pension formula.

Career Counseling: Career transition counseling will be available for all employees. Retirement seminars will be offered as an alternative to those eligible for pension enhancement.

Financial Counseling: Financial counseling will be offered to all employees.

Health Benefits: The first six months of medical and dental benefits will be provided to all employees after their termination date.

Any employee with questions about the severance package or who would like further information, should feel free to contact the manager of benefits and employee relations at ext. 957.

8-7: Elimination of Position

To: Sam Pearson

Fr: Human Resources Manager

Re: Elimination of Position

Over the past year the Company has seen a dramatic change in its business. We have acquired new processes which have streamlined our plant and shortened the time it takes to make our products. We have also acquired new customers with different, often simpler, product lines than those we have manufactured in the past. Because of these changes, we no longer have the same staffing needs.

We have evaluated all of our positions and concluded that some are no longer necessary. The job you do is one in which we now find that we have too many people for the available workload. The workforce in your area must be reduced by 20 people.

This has left us with the difficult task of deciding who we must lay off. We have assessed each individual in your job class in relation to their seniority and performance. I regret to inform you that your job is one of the 20 being eliminated. You will be laid off as of today.

To help ease this difficult change, and to assist you with your transition as you seek another job, we will provide you with the following resources:

- Severance pay in the amount of two weeks regular wages;
- Payment for double your accrued vacation time;
- A referral to Manderly Outplacement Center. This includes a 4-hour job search course and 4 hours of personal job search counseling;
- A letter of reference from your supervisor;

8-7:   Elimination of Position (continued)

■   A $500 credit at the Technology Center good for any training
    classes you choose to take to better prepare you for another job.

Additionally, you may apply for unemployment insurance at the state
job service office. A listing of their locations in the area is attached.
The amount of your benefit is dependent on your past earnings. We
have informed their office of this layoff, and one of the case managers
will be glad to assist you in completing the required paperwork to
obtain this benefit.

Should our situation change in the future and we find we need to hire
additional workers, you and the others who have been laid off will be
eligible for recall into a job for which you are qualified. Your
application will remain on an active status for the next 12 months, and
we will notify you of any openings. Should you be rehired, you would
have your seniority reinstated after one year of service.

Sam, you have been a valued employee to our company and we truly
regret the need for this action. We wish you the best of luck. Please let
us know if there is anything else we can do to assist you during this
transition.

8-8:   General Announcement of Layoffs

To: All Employees

Fr: Human Resources Manager

Re: Layoffs

Due to changes in our manufacturing processes and new customers with
different demands, we recently determined that we were overstaffed.

8-8: General Announcement of Layoffs (continued)

All positions were assessed and the number of people in each job class evaluated. Through this process it became evident that we needed to eliminate 20 jobs in the fabrication division.

Those who are being laid off have been notified. Every effort is being made to assist them in finding other employment. Should our situation change, these people will be eligible for recall to fill new positions.

We truly regret the need for this action, but felt it was necessary to maintain our business. Based on our current understanding of the markets and our company, we do not anticipate any further layoffs at this time. We believe we are now poised to succeed as we adapt to changes in our business environment.

We realize a change like this affects everyone. If you have concerns about the handling of the situation, the treatment if those who are being laid off, the security of your own job, or any other concerns or questions, please come talk to me or any of the other managers. We want to continue the open communications that have always characterized our company. Together we will weather this difficult transition and keep the company a great place to work.

Misconduct, Reprimand and Termination Letters

9-1:   Reprimand--Violation of Drug Abuse Policy

Dear Ms. Baxter:

In compliance with our drug-free workforce policy implementation procedure, you were required to submit to a random drug analysis screening last week. The analysis has been completed and the results indicate that illegal substances were present in your system (a positive result).

Because this is your first violation of the drug policy, the company believes you should have the opportunity to correct your behavior. You will be allowed to continue your employment with *Langley, Inc.* provided you agree to the following terms:

1. You will be suspended from work for a period of five working days. During this time you will enroll in a rehabilitation program and begin meeting with a substance abuse counselor. You will not return to work until the counselor has made a recommendation and a negative drug test has been received.

2. You must successfully complete the rehabilitation program for substance abuse. Information and referrals concerning local treatment facilities will be provided by the company's substance abuse coordinator.

3. Urinalysis screens will be conducted as a part of your rehabilitation treatment program. Screening intervals will be designated by the company. Communication with your treatment counselor will be continuous throughout your treatment.

9-1:   Reprimand--Violation of Drug Abuse Policy (continued)

4. Subsequent urinalysis screens will be performed to further detect if illegal substances are still present in your system. Screening will be on a random basis within 30 days of completion of your treatment program, then on a quarterly basis thereafter for a period of one year.

5. Failure to successfully complete a rehabilitation program, or testing positive during or after the completion of a program, will result in the immediate termination of your employment. Employees must remain drug free during the course of their treatment. Any employee who fails to complete an assigned rehabilitation program and is subsequently terminated, will not be given the option of voluntary resignation.

6. If you choose not to participate in a rehabilitation program, you will have the option to resign in lieu of termination.

We strive to provide all our employees with a safe, healthy, and pleasant working environment that is free of substance abuse. During these next crucial weeks and months, your complete support and compliance in this effort is expected.

If you have any questions concerning the conditions outlined, or would like to discuss your screening results, please feel free to contact me at (219) 420-xxxx.

Sincerely,

9-2:   Termination--Violation of Drug Abuse Policy

Dear Mr. Marshall:

You have violated the drug and substance abuse policy of *Taylor Temporary Services*. Effective immediately, your employment is being terminated.

After observing your odd behavior yesterday, your supervisor began to suspect you were under the influence of drugs. You were immediately sent to an off-site facility for testing. The results of that test indicate there were high levels of illegal drugs in your bloodstream.

The company has communicated to all employees on numerous occasions that it will not tolerate the use of illegal drugs or the abuse of legal drugs and alcohol. The company policy is to terminate those who violate the policy.

Human Resources is waiting to discuss your COBRA benefits with you. Please return your keycard and ID to HR and make an appointment to pick up your personal belongings.

Sincerely,

9-3:   Response to Request to Continue Employment

Dear Mr. Swanson:

On August 3, we met to discuss your pending termination. You had requested the meeting because you believed there were extenuating circumstances of which we were not aware. At the end of the meeting you asked if we would reconsider keeping you on staff.

This letter is to inform you that we have reached a decision concerning the continuance of your employment. After evaluating the events

9-3: Response to Request to Continue Employment (continued)

surrounding the issuance of the termination request by your manager, we cannot reasonably dispute this action. You were placed on a six-month probationary period effective February 7, at which time you were notified that any further misconduct would result in the immediate loss of your job. On July 31, you violated the company's drug and substance abuse policy.

This decision is final. You will be extended the opportunity to voluntarily resign in lieu of termination.

Sincerely,

9-4: Notification of Impending Termination

Dear Ms. Dixon:

Unfortunately, you have failed to comply with the company's request that you return to work immediately. This request was made because your approved disability period ended over one week ago.

The records of your physician and the consulting firm monitoring your treatment indicate that you are now well enough to return to work full-time. Since your continuing absence is without basis, you are directed to report for work on Monday, March 12. If you fail to report, we will consider your job abandoned and will terminate your employment at the close of business on Monday.

If you have any questions, or there is anything you wish to bring to our attention, please call me as soon as possible at: 615-285-xxxx.

Sincerely,

9-5: Administrative Discharge

Dear Mr. Brennan:

This letter is to inform you that as of February 19, you have been administratively discharged. This action has been taken because you have been in a layoff status over the allotted period of time.

If you wish to be reconsidered for employment, you must come to the Human Resources department and reapply.

If you have any questions, please give me a call at (408) 217-xxxx.

Sincerely,

9-6: Administrative Termination

Dear Mr. Anderson:

We are aware of your recent illness and hope you will soon recover. Unfortunately, during your absence we have had to hire additional personnel in order to meet our current production schedule. As a result, your employment has been terminated.

Your termination will become effective on June 15. Please contact the Human Resources department at your earliest convenience to schedule an exit interview. At that time you will be required to return all company property including badges, tools, keys, etc.

You are welcome to submit a new application to Human Resources if you would like to be considered for future employment. Should you have any questions, don't hesitate to contact me at (817) 774-xxxx.

Sincerely,

9-7: Termination for Misconduct

Dear Ms. Reid:

On July 22 we met to discuss the latest incidents in which you were involved while in the office last Friday, July 19. Specifically, you were seen drinking alcoholic beverages and sleeping on the job.

From our preliminary investigation we learned that these occurrences were witnessed by several people, including your manager and other workers in your department. All said that you were drinking openly, became intoxicated then later passed out at your desk. You are well aware that such conduct is unacceptable and violates company policy.

Following the July 22 meeting you were placed on suspension without pay until the events could be investigated further. The purpose of this letter is to inform you that the investigation is now complete.

Your history with the company, particularly during the past year, has been filled with episodes like this latest one. In the last nine months you have received four written warnings for unauthorized absenteeism, tardiness, and poor productivity. You have been given any number of opportunities to correct your behavior, but to date you have chosen not to do so.

Based on the evidence in this most recent case, and your numerous past violations of company policy, the decision has been made to terminate your employment effective immediately.

Sincerely,

9-8: Final Warning for Sexual Harassment

Dear Mr. Allan:

This is the notice of a final written warning for several violations of the company's policy prohibiting sexual harassment. A copy of this notice will be placed in a confidential, limited access personnel file.

The specific acts you committed which are in violation of the policy were:

1. Touching another employee in a suggestive manner;

2. Making sexually suggestive comments and remarks; and

3. Using coercion to obtain sexual favors.

The company considers these violations extremely serious. Further violations of the policy against sexual harassment involving this or any other employee could result in the immediate termination of your employment.

This final written warning is effective for one year from its date.

Sincerely,

9-9: Warning for Failure to Report Sexual Harassment

Dear Bill:

I am very disappointed to learn that your were aware of the complaints of sexual harassment made by Katherine Paige against David Fletcher. In spite of this knowledge, you failed to report the matter to senior management or to take any action whatsoever.

Behavior such as Mr. Fletcher's is inappropriate in the workplace and will not be tolerated by this company. As a manager, you have an obligation to enforce our policy against sexual harassment. As such, you were obligated to make me aware of this situation. Your failure to do so has resulted in the issuance of this written warning.

It is also your responsibility to help enforce the company's policy against retaliation. Should you observe or learn of any adverse action taken against Ms. Paige, or any other employee involved in the investigation, you must report it to me immediately.

A copy of our sexual harassment policy is attached. You are expected to be familiar with all of its terms and to enforce them at all times. Your failure to do so in the future regarding Mr. Fletcher, or any other employee, will result in severe disciplinary action, up to and including termination.

Sincerely,

9-10: Disciplinary Suspension and Final Warning for Sexual Harassment

Dear Mr. Fletcher:

This is to inform you that effective November 7 through November 20 you are suspended without pay. You are to return to work on November 21, according to your regular schedule.

This suspension is in response to the complaints that I received regarding the inappropriate language and behavior that you exhibited toward Katherine Paige and other employees. This type of language violates our policy against sexual harassment and will not be tolerated. Moreover, in conducting the investigation of this complaint, I learned that you treat many of your employees, both male and female, in a disrespectful, belittling and unprofessional manner.

I have reviewed the sexual harassment policy in detail with you. I have also attached a copy of it to this warning to assure that you fully understand your obligations under the policy.

You must change the manner in which you speak to, and treat, your employees immediately if you wish to continue your employment with the company. This is a ***final warning***. If you engage in the same or similar misconduct in the future, you will be immediately discharged. Further, you are prohibited against taking any retaliatory action against Ms. Paige or any other employee who participated in the investigation.

Sincerely,

9-11: Performance Problems--Second Warning

Dear Leslie:

On August 23, you were given a warning concerning your performance. You had failed to follow procedures for inputting and checking inventories into the computer system. Since that warning approximately one year ago, you have continued to have performance problems. Specifically, you still have not been following correct procedures.

Attached is a list of open purchase orders from several months ago. You were asked to check these and ensure that they had been handled correctly. When I examined the purchase orders I found that you had stamped them as input, but you had not actually entered them into the computer. Not only does this mean you stamped them out of sequence, but it also indicates you did not check them against the computer print out as procedures require.

Leslie, your performance must improve immediately. You are being placed on probation for the next 60 days. During that time you will be given every bit of help and assistance you request. I will do all I can to help you, but you must show improvement and have no further incidents of this kind. If the problem continues and you do not show the needed improvement, further action will be taken, including possible termination or relocation within the company.

==

I have read and understand this warning. I have also received a copy for my records.

_____   _____
Signature   Date

9-12: Performance Problems--Quality of Work

Dear Peter:

You received a written warning on September 22, regarding the quality of your work. You were told that your performance would be reviewed in 60 days. During that 60-day period your work was to be error free. Since that time you have had two additional work errors, one on November 10 and one on November 18. This is unacceptable work quality.

You are being suspended without pay for the remainder of today and the rest of this week. During this time we will evaluate whether or not you should continue to work for the company. You should also take this time to consider whether you feel you can work here and perform at an acceptable quality level.

If you are allowed to return on Monday, you will have to work for a minimum of 90 days with NO work errors. If you have another error within this period, you may be terminated. Further disciplinary action may also be taken if you have errors after the 90 days expire.

Peter, we would like you to succeed in this job. We will help in any way we can, but in the end it is up to you to change and to approach your work with greater care.

===

I have read and understand this warning. I have also received a copy for my records.

_____   _____

Signature   Date

9-13: Termination--Falsification of Records

Dear Mark:

On June 13, you were scheduled to begin work at 5 AM and had been asked to act as the lead person for the crew that day. You were asked to take this leadership position due to your seniority, and because you had been trained and had acted in this role in the past.

Upon review of your timecard and those of your crew for that day, it became apparent to your lead and supervisor that you had made several inaccurate entries to timecards:

1. You punched in late yourself, then crossed through your punched in time and wrote in 5 AM.

2. A fellow employee came to work at approximately 5:45 AM. You did not have her punch in when she arrived and wrote in her starting time as 5 AM. We were able to verify her actual starting time through several credible eye witnesses.

3. Another employee also did not punch in and you wrote in his starting time as 5 AM. We were unable to verify his actual start time, but know that it was after 5 AM.

These actions constitute falsification of company records, and are a direct violation of company policy. They are considered grounds for immediate termination. Our policy specifically states: "Unauthorized punching or recording of another employee's timecard is an action which may result in immediate discharge." You are aware of the policy, have been given a copy of it, and it has been explained to you by your supervisor.

We have reviewed your personnel record and found that there was another instance of a severe violation of company policy just last year. You have also received numerous warnings for poor attendance in the past. This, combined with this most recent violation, has led us to conclude that your employment should be terminated immediately.

9-14: Performance Warning--Letter to Employee's File

As supervisor of the extrusion department, I have been working closely with Victor Abbott in the last few months as he has been learning his new job in the die shop. From my observation of his work during this time I noticed he was constantly making mistakes. These errors, in my opinion, should not have been made by anyone who has been doing this job longer than one month. The mistakes I speak of include:

- mounting the dies up wrong;
- mistagging the dies;
- not taking the dies out of the hot box;
- not putting the dies in the hot box when they were supposed to go in;
- taking an excessive amount of time to mount the dies.

Such mistakes will hurt the quality and productivity of the extrusion department.   In my mind they are mistakes that cannot be tolerated.

On January 25, the department head asked me and another department supervisor to meet with him and Victor. The purpose of the meeting was to discuss the mistakes and how they could be corrected. Victor was very defensive during the meeting. We were trying to help him, but he appeared to take the attitude that we did not have the right to tell him about his mistakes. After the meeting I told the department head that since Victor seemed so unwilling to listen, I doubted he would be able to perform his duties in the die shop in a satisfactory manner.

9-15: Request for Demotion--Letter to Employee's File

This is to document my reasons for requesting the transfer of Victor Abbott out of the die shop.

Four months ago Victor was promoted to train as a die chaser in the die shop. From the very beginning he has not been able to perform most of the tasks he has been trained and assigned to do in an accurate manner.

The first week of January, due to continued problems with his performance, it was necessary for me to have a one-on-one meeting with Victor. We discussed the lead people's concern with his work, and we briefly talked about his inability to perform the rest of his job responsibilities. After a conversation involving expressed opinions on both sides, it was apparent Victor was not willing to accept my observations that he was having a problem. I informed him that his performance must improve immediately.

This is now the third week in January and the problems have not diminished. In fact, they have increased. A second meeting was called with Victor. This time I invited the lead people in extrusion so they could speak directly to Victor and explain their concerns. The meeting lasted about 30 minutes and again Victor disagreed with our assessment of his mistakes and inabilities to perform the duties of die chaser.

It is my conclusion that Victor is unable to learn the duties of this new position. He is unwilling to take input from me and the others he works with regarding his need for improvement. Victor has been successful in the other positions he held prior to this job. I believe it would be in his best interest and the best interest of the company to transfer him immediately into his previous position.

9-16: Attendance Warning

To: Len Myerson

Fr: Human Resources Manager

Re: Attendance

Len, on June 7 your manager gave you a warning about your attendance. At that time you had 5 1/2 absences. As you know, we usually terminate employees who have 5 absences in a six-month period.

Because of the special circumstances in your case, we gave you another chance to show your reliability. We excused one of the absences, lowering the total to 4 1/2, and told you that for the next three months you could not be late or absent. On August 23, you called in sick. This brought your number of absences back up to 5 1/2.

Len, we realize you have some on-going health concerns but this attendance record is unacceptable. We cannot continue to make exceptions to the company's policies for you. This would not be fair to the rest of our employees.

I have spoken your manager and he has agreed that we will give you one final chance to improve your attendance record. If you do not follow these guidelines, we will have no choice but to let you go:

1. You will have to work until November 1 without being late or absent. By that time you will no longer be on warning for attendance.

2. If your are late or absent before November 1, you may be terminated.

3. If you continue to go back on attendance warning after November 1, we may also consider further discipline and/or termination.

9-16: Attendance Warning (continued)

All of us who work with you value the contributions you make to the company when you are here, Len. We don't want to lose you. But we do have to draw the line somewhere to be fair and consistent with everyone.

Please do everything you can to improve your attendance record so no further action will be necessary.

===

I have read and understand this warning. I have also received a copy for my records.

_____   _____

Signature   Date

9-17: Performance Warning--Excessive Mistakes

Dear Suzanne:

Since you began working in the customer service department, there have been a number of instances in which you have made mistakes. Some of these mistakes have been very serious in terms of the costs to the company. They have also had a negative impact on our customers.

Each time these mistakes have been made, I have brought them to your attention. We discussed what was done wrong and what you must do differently in the future. We have spent a great deal of time going over correct procedures and ensuring that you know how to follow them. At

9-17: Performance Problems--Errors (continued)

the end of every meeting you have agreed to follow the procedures and to change behavior as I have asked. Yet, you still continue to make many of the same mistakes over and over.

After thoroughly reviewing your performance, it appears to me that most of these mistakes are not due to a lack of knowledge regarding procedures. Instead, most have been mistakes in which you did not take the time to follow the procedures. This shows me that with more attention to detail, greater conscientiousness and better organization, you are quite capable of performing these duties.

The seriousness of your performance problems has reached the point where I must inform you that you may be removed from this position if your performance does not improve dramatically and immediately. Attached is a list detailing the specific behaviors that must be followed from now on. As you will see, we have discussed them all before and we will discuss them in detail again. I will give you whatever help, training, feedback and assistance I can. You, however, must take responsibility for making the necessary changes.

I will continue to work with you for the next thirty (30) days on these issues. At the end of that time period, or prior to that if needed, we will meet again formally and evaluate your performance. If you have not significantly improved by that time, or if there are indications before then that you are not making adequate effort or are unable to improve, I will need to take further action, including possible termination.

Suzanne, I believe you have a great deal of potential and are very capable of succeeding in this position. I would like to see you continue in the department. My intent in pointing out these problems to you is to help you, if you are willing, to turn around your performance. Please view this as an opportunity to become better and more successful at your job.

9-17: Performance Problems--Errors (continued)

Performance Changes--Specific Behaviors Required of Suzanne Briggs

Task-Specific Behaviors

1. Legibly write down orders received by phone and verify the information with the customer while he/she is still on the line. Pay particular attention to: a) customer number; b) correct drop ship number; c) purchase order numbers.

2. When you enter orders on the screen: a) ALWAYS view the comment file; b) ALWAYS confirm the quantity, description, and ship date on the screen against your actual order form; c) verify special pricing and additional discounts.

Organizational Behaviors

1. Organize your desk so that all of the catalogs, order forms, phone message pads, telephone indexes, etc., are easily accessible.

2. Use your planner to organize your daily tasks, note the calls you need to make, record conversations or important points you need to remember. ALWAYS call back customers when you say you will.

3. When you are given an assignment, ask questions if you do not understand it thoroughly. Listen carefully to instructions.

Interpersonal Behaviors

1. Talk to customers in a more courteous and professional manner. Mirror how they speak to you.

2. Be flexible if conditions arise that may make it necessary for you to leave for lunch later or stay a bit after 5 PM.

3. If a mistake has been made with a customer, display empathy. Convey that we will do whatever is necessary to make things right.

10

Letters on Special Topics

10-1: Diversity Awareness and Training

INTEROFFICE MEMORANDUM

Subject: DIVERSITY INITIATIVE

Date: October 15, 19xx

To: All Employees

From: President and CEO

I am pleased to announce that after a year of planning, we are beginning the first phase of our diversity initiative. Many of you participated in focus groups and provided input and we are pleased with the outcome.

Learning to value and respect differences are critical to our success if we want to remain competitive. Differences, whether race, gender or age, are one of the first things we recognize about our co-workers and our customers. We must learn to value those differences as we prepare to do business with a more diverse group of individuals.

Over the next several months, all employees will attend diversity training seminars to make them more aware of diversity issues and how to work with people of different backgrounds. All non-management employees will attend a one-day program. Management personnel will attend an extended program which includes a second day of training. On day two managers will learn how to apply the information on evaluating, mentoring and working with employees from diverse backgrounds presented on the first day.

10-1: Diversity Awareness and Training (continued)

Each month, we will hold brown bag workshops at lunchtime focusing on diversity topics such as ethnic differences, gay and lesbian issues and age issues. Please plan to attend these over the next few months. In November, the cafeteria will feature different ethnic foods each day during the weeks of November 8 and November 15.

I am very excited about this initiative and hope you will fully participate. We will be asking employees to help in planning other activities. I hope to see you at the programs over the months to come.

10-2: Contribution to Non-Profit Organization

Dear Ms. Carpenter:

Allied Industries is pleased to present you with the enclosed donation of $6,000 for your new Madison county facility. We believe this will provide adequate funds to upgrade the furnishings in the leadership training room.

The Technology Center has provided a number of training services to our organization over the years. This contribution is our way of showing our appreciation and continued support of your organization. We are especially excited about the new facility which will be a much more convenient location for our classes.

Our general manager and I look forward to the open house on March 2. If there is anything else we can do, let us know. Again, please accept this donation with our thanks and best wishes for the success of the new facility.

Sincerely,

10-3:   Diversity Commitment

To: All Employees

Fr: Human Resources

Re: Company's Commitment to Diversity

Our company is committed to being a leader in the market place and providing a quality work environment for all of its employees.

Being a leader means taking advantage of the talents and contributions of all employees. Differences among our employees based on race, gender, age, national origin, disability status, or religion are sources of strength for our company, and all employees are encouraged to take advantage of the opportunities our differences provide.

Achieving a quality work environment includes having all managers, supervisors, and employees take responsibility for showing mutual respect and understanding to all employees. This means every employee should work to eliminate unfair or prejudicial stereotypes.

We encourage all employees to learn more about the company's diversity commitment by reading the attached booklet, *Diversity at Sinclair Publishing* and attending the upcoming company-sponsored training programs on the subject of diversity.

Everyone's support of our diversity efforts is expected and appreciated.

10-4:   General Release

Dear Ms. Holder:

Outlined below are the terms of a general release agreement with *Quantum Technologies*. You should thoroughly review and understand the terms and their effects before taking any action. Please consider the release for at least ten (10) days. During this time you are also encouraged to consult with an attorney prior to deciding to sign it.

In consideration of the benefits offered to you under the company's enhanced separation program, you agree to release and discharge *Quantum Technologies,* its affiliates, parents, successors, predecessors, subsidiaries, and assigns, (hereinafter referred to as "The Company") from all claims and/or causes of action, known or unknown, which you may have or claim to have against the Company arising from or during your employment or as a result of the termination of your employment. You hereby agree not to sue the Company on any such claim or cause of action. This release includes but is not limited to the claims arising under federal, state or local laws prohibiting employment discrimination based upon age, race, sex, religion, handicap, national origin or any other impermissible characteristic including but not limited to any and all claims arising under the *Age Discrimination in Employment Act* and *Title VII* of the *Civil Rights Act of 1964,* or claims growing out of any legal restrictions, expressed or implied, on the Company's right to terminate the employment of its employees.

By signing below you acknowledge that you have carefully read and fully understand the provisions of this General Release and you have had sufficient time and opportunity to consult with an attorney prior to signing it. You further acknowledge that you are signing this General Release knowingly and voluntarily and without duress, coercion or undue influence. This Agreement and the separation policy constitute the entire understanding between you and the Company relating to the subject matter covered by this General Release.

Signature:_____   Date_____

10-5:   Last Chance Agreement & Waiver of Rights

This Last Chance Agreement is entered into as of the 25th day of February, 19xx by and between Tupelo Steel ("Company"), Patrick Ryan ("Ryan") and QBC Local 123 ("Union").

The Company, Ryan and the Union hereby agree as follows:

1. The Company agrees to allow Ryan to return to work effective February 26, 19xx.

2. In return for his reinstatement to work, Ryan will:

a. participate in and successfully complete the treatment and rehabilitation program for drug and/or alcohol abuse in which he is currently enrolled;

b. furnish documentation satisfactory to the Company of his attendance and successful completion of the treatment and rehabilitation program in which he is currently enrolled; and

c. voluntarily submit to medical testing at any time, within the Company's discretion, to determine whether he has consumed or used, or whether he is under the influence of, alcohol or any illegal drug or illegal substance.

3. Ryan further agrees that:

a. if he refuses or fails to cooperate in the aforementioned treatment, he will be discharged immediately;

b. if he fails to submit to medical testing, or if he fails to provide the Company with a report and results of such testing, he will be discharged immediately;

c. if the results of the medical testing indicate that he has consumed or used or is under the influence of alcohol or any illegal drug or substance, he will be discharged immediately.

10-5: Last Chance Agreement (continued)

4. Ryan and the Union agree that this is Ryan's last chance. Any violation of this Agreement shall result in his termination. In such event, the only issue subject to grievance procedure of Section 13 of the Collective Bargaining Agreement, if grieved, shall be the question of whether Ryan violated this Agreement; the issue of whether discharge is an appropriate penalty shall not be grievable or arbitrable.

5. Ryan and the Union waive any and all rights to file and/or pursue grievance or any other complaints, claims and/or charges which either Ryan or the Union may have had, has or may have arising from Ryan's employment to date with the Company and/or challenging the terms of this Last Chance Agreement and/or relating to any events prior to its execution before any federal, state, local or private court, agency, arbitrator or other entity under any contract, federal, state or local law, statute, common law, regulation or ordinance, on any theory of any nature whatsoever.

6. Ryan agrees that the Union has fairly represented him in this entire matter.

7. Ryan, the Union and the Company acknowledge, declare and represent that they fully understand the terms of this Last Chance Agreement and Waiver of Rights, that they each had an adequate opportunity to review the document, and that no promise, inducement or agreement has been made except as expressly provided in this Last Chance Agreement and Waiver of Rights, that this document contains the entire agreement between the parties, and that each party has voluntarily and knowingly signed this Last Chance Agreement and Waiver of Rights.

10-5: Last Chance Agreement (continued)

IN WITNESS HEREOF, each of the parties hereto, either individually or by its duly authorized representative(s), has signed this Last Chance Agreement and Waiver of Rights on the date indicated.

Patrick Ryan   QBC Local 123

_____   _____

Date: _____   Date: _____

Tupelo Steel

_____

Date:_____

10-6: Response to Attorney Requesting Employee File

Dear Mr. Martin:

We have received your letter requesting a copy of Alan Parker's personnel file. We understand you are currently counseling Mr. Parker on his recent termination from our company.

Our company's policy is to keep all personnel records confidential. Since state law does not require private employers to disclose personnel files, we do not feel it is necessary to provide you with a copy of our records at this time.

10-6: Response: Attorney Requesting Employee File (continued)

Every employee is given a copy of the corporate policy manual at the time of his/her hire. Mr. Parker also received a copy of this manual, which should include the information you have requested.

As stated in the letter given to Mr. Parker at the time of his termination, his blatant insubordination was considered grounds for immediate dismissal. Several peers, as well as his supervisor, attested to the fact that he used abusive language toward his superiors and openly stated his refusal to recognize their authority. This type of behavior cannot be tolerated in our business.

Sincerely,

10-7: Account for Flowers

To: All Employees

Fr: Human Resources

There have been some questions recently as to when the company sends flowers. Just to remind everyone, the company has set up an account to send flowers to employees only under these circumstances:

- when the employee is in the hospital;
- when the employee's spouse or child(ren) is hospitalized;
- when the employee or the employee's spouse has a baby;
- when a member of the employee's immediate family (spouse, children, mother, father, grandparents, brother, sister, in-laws) passes away.

It is up to each department supervisor to contact Purchasing when one of these events occurs so the flowers can be sent.

10-8: Reference for Employee Arrested for DUI

To Whom It May Concern:

Christine Reese has been employed full time with *Cranston Industries* since May 25, 1983. She works in our packing department and is currently a lead over a crew of eighteen workers.

I have worked with Chris for the past four years. During that time I have found her to be a very responsible, dependable employee. She is in a key leadership position and would not be there if we did not have a great deal of trust in her ability. She always conveys a positive, helpful attitude to all people with whom she works.

I understand Chris has recently been arrested for driving under the influence of alcohol. Our company in no way condones such activity and we have a strict drug/alcohol policy. From my personal interactions with Chris, I feel this incident is not characteristic of her usual behavior, nor will it be a recurring problem. I believe Chris is quite responsible, but she made a mistake and I know she will learn from it.

We value the contributions Chris makes to our company and hope this problem can be resolved so she will be able to continue working here. We provide an assistance program to all employees, and Chris has told me she is willing to utilize it fully to bring this matter to a satisfactory close. I have also expressed to Chris that if there is anything we can do as her employer to help her, within the bounds of our company policies, we will make every effort.

If you have further questions concerning Chris's employment or her performance her at work, please feel free to contact me at 201-732-xxxx.

Sincerely,

10-9: Response to Attorney--Insurance Claim

Dear Mr. Barnes:

Your request for information concerning Lynne Clybourne's
employment with *TDC Manufacturing, Inc.,* has been forwarded to me.
Our company's procedure is to have these types of question answered
directly through the HR office instead of by the employee's supervisor,
who is quite busy on a daily basis. Further, I am in a better position to
respond to your questions, since I dealt directly with Ms. Clybourne
myself on her termination. I will try to address each question listed in
your letter.   If you need additional information, please contact me at
218-961-xxxx.

Ms. Clybourne was employed with *TDC* on 10/4/89 as a fabrication
machine operator. She was in that position until her termination on
7/5/94. Her duties included processing long strips of aluminum trim
through various machines that punched, bent, and cut metal for the final
product. The job requires employees to lift/move/exert pressure of 50
pounds regularly and up to 100 pounds on occasion.

Ms. Clybourne worked an average of 40 hours per week, which is
normal for all our employees. At that time we were not requiring any
overtime in our fabrication department, but there was one week in a
three-month period prior to her accident when Lynne did work two
hours of overtime. Her rate of pay during the three months before her
accident was $9.17 per hour.

When Ms. Clybourne had her accident, she first used all her sick leave
then her vacation time toward her time off. This paid her through May
1 at her regular rate of pay. She then requested and was granted an
unpaid leave of absence. Our policy states that employees can take such
a leave, but will not be guaranteed their same position if they return on
the agreed upon date. They will not be guaranteed any job at all if they
return as agreed and there are no openings, or if they come back after
the set return date. The policy also states that after 60 days of absence,
an employee will be terminated unless he/she has a pre-arranged

10-9: Response--Insurance Claim (continued)

agreement with management specifying a date of return.

I spoke regularly with Ms. Clybourne about her intent to return to work. She reported that her condition remained such that she could not perform her previous job. She also said her doctor estimated she would need to remain off the job an additional four to six months, but there would still be no way to determine when or IF she would ever be able to return to work, even on a less strenuous job.

Because of this uncertainty and our need to have Ms. Clybourne's vacant position filled, I decided to follow our policy and terminate her employment effective 7/5/94. I told Ms. Clybourne that whenever she was released by her doctor to return to work, we would make every attempt to find a position for her and she would be given preference over any other applicants pending our hiring needs at the time. Her termination was due solely to her medical condition and she left on good terms. She was fully eligible for rehire if she was able to do her job again in the future. I have not heard from Ms. Clybourne regarding any change in her status or her desire to be rehired since that time.

Prior to her accident, Ms. Clybourne was a capable performer in fabrication. She occasionally had some interpersonal difficulties with others in the department, but overall was an acceptable employee. She was making improvements in her weak areas and there would have been no reason for her termination other than her medical situation as the result of her accident. Her attendance was not exceptional, but was well within our guidelines for acceptability. She did take some vacation time in January for surgery, but there is no record of the nature of the surgery. In reviewing her attendance record for the six months prior to the accident it appears she called in sick every other month for one or two days each time. This is probably average for our hourly employees.

I hope this information will help you in resolving Ms. Clybourne's claims. If I can be of further assistance, please call.

Sincerely,

10-10: Letter of Reference--Independent Contractor

To Whom It May Concern:

Tracy Scott has been associated with *Jennings Limited* for last ten years as a store service representative. In this role she has represented our company to all the Krammer office supply stores in the Albany, New York area. Her duties include taking orders from store managers, communicating orders to our offices, tracking inventory in store displays, assisting the stores with needed marketing/product information and handling any subsequent questions or problems.

In all of her dealings with our customers, Tracy has represented *Jennings* in an outstanding manner. She is friendly, organized, hard working and reliable. She makes sure the right product is in its place when promised, so neither the stores nor our company have to worry. If a problem does arise, she quickly does whatever it takes to ensure the matter is resolved to the customer's satisfaction and beyond.

Recently, *Jennings Limited* was awarded the "Vendor of the Year" award from Krammer. While we realize that providing quality products and services takes the efforts of people throughout the country, we know that Tracy played the largest role in our receiving that award. Tracy *is Jennings* to most of the people at Krammer, and we are proud that she has given them such an outstanding impression of our company.

I have worked with Tracy for years and have always been pleased with the excellent job she does. I highly recommend her for any other product lines or companies she chooses to represent in the future. I would be happy to discuss her qualifications by phone, if desired.

Tracy has been an outstanding representative for us, and we are proud to have her as part of the *Jennings* team.

Sincerely,

10-11: Letter of Reference--Student Intern

To Whom It May Concern:

Tanika Knight has worked for *Crystal Communications* since June 2, 1994 as a training specialist intern. This is a temporary position in the Human Resources department for the summer months. The main responsibilities of the job are to develop a training course titled "Team Dynamics" for our employees. This course helps people learn how to work in teams by understanding the stages of growth teams go through, the roles individuals play in teams, the communication process, listening skills, conflict resolution and meeting management skills.

The course is eight hours, and Tanika has had sole responsibility for its development. She has designed the course content, developed the instructor and participant materials, and organized all materials. She will soon teach the course to a pilot group then evaluate its effectiveness. This is a huge assignment and Tanika has done an excellent job.

During the time Tanika has worked here, I have found her to be very professional, creative, and organized. She designed an exceptional course and sought input from people throughout the company to ensure it met the needs of the participants. Her ability to communicate with people at all levels have earned her a great deal of respect.

I have not worked with Tanika long but because of the intensity of the project, I have worked with her quite closely. I feel confident in recommending her for any position that requires a creative, organized employee with a very positive attitude. Because of her excellent communication skills, she would work well in a leadership role. I would especially recommend her for positions which involve training and educating people.

If you have any questions concerning Tanika's performance here, I would be happy to speak with you in person or by phone. You may reach me at 315-724-xxxx.

Sincerely,

INDEX

TITLES OF INTEREST IN MARKETING, DIRECT MARKETING, AND SALES PROMOTION

SUCCESSFUL DIRECT MARKETING METHODS, by Bob Stone
PROFITABLE DIRECT MARKETING, by Jim Kobs
INTEGRATED DIRECT MARKETING, by Ernan Roman
BEYOND 2000: THE FUTURE OF DIRECT MARKETING, by Jerry I. Reitman
POWER DIRECT MARKETING, by "Rocket" Ray Jutkins
CREATIVE STRATEGY IN DIRECT MARKETING, by Susan K. Jones
SECRETS OF SUCCESSFUL DIRECT MAIL, by Richard V. Benson
STRATEGIC DATABASE MARKETING, by Rob Jackson and Paul Wang
SUCCESSFUL TELEMARKETING, by Bob Stone and John Wyman
BUSINESS TO BUSINESS DIRECT MARKETING, by Robert Bly
COMMONSENSE DIRECT MARKETING, by Drayton Bird
DIRECT MARKETING CHECKLISTS, by John Stockwell and Henry Shaw
INTEGRATED MARKETING COMMUNICATIONS, by Don E. Schultz, Stanley I. Tannenbaum, and Robert F. Lauterborn
NEW DIRECTIONS IN MARKETING, by Aubrey Wilson
GREEN MARKETING, by Jacquelyn Ottman
MARKETING CORPORATE IMAGE: THE COMPANY AS YOUR NUMBER ONE PRODUCT, by James R. Gregory with Jack G. Wiechmann
HOW TO CREATE SUCCESSFUL CATALOGS, by Maxwell Sroge
101 TIPS FOR MORE PROFITABLE CATALOGS, by Maxwell Sroge
SALES PROMOTION ESSENTIALS, by Don E. Schultz, William A. Robinson and Lisa A. Petrison
PROMOTIONAL MARKETING, by William A. Robinson and Christine Hauri
BEST SALES PROMOTIONS, by William A. Robinson
INSIDE THE LEADING MAIL ORDER HOUSES, by Maxwell Sroge
NEW PRODUCT DEVELOPMENT, by George Gruenwald
NEW PRODUCT DEVELOPMENT CHECKLISTS, by George Gruenwald
CLASSIC FAILURES IN PRODUCT MARKETING, by Donald W. Hendon
HOW TO TURN CUSTOMER SERVICE INTO CUSTOMER SALES, by Bernard Katz
ADVERTISING & MARKETING CHECKLISTS, by Ron Kaatz
BRAND MARKETING, by William M. Weilbacher
MARKETING WITHOUT MONEY, by Nicholas E. Bade
THE 1-DAY MARKETING PLAN, by Roman A. Hiebing, Jr. and Scott W. Cooper
HOW TO WRITE A SUCCESSFUL MARKETING PLAN, by Roman G. Hiebing, Jr. and Scott W. Cooper
DEVELOPING, IMPLEMENTING, AND MANAGING EFFECTIVE MARKETING PLANS, by Hal Goetsch
HOW TO EVALUATE AND IMPROVE YOUR MARKETING DEPARTMENT, by Keith Sparling and Gerard Earls
SELLING TO A SEGMENTED MARKET, by Chester A. Swenson
MARKET-ORIENTED PRICING, by Michael Morris and Gene Morris
STATE-OF-THE-ART MARKETING RESEARCH, by A.B. Blankenship and George E. Breen
AMA HANDBOOK FOR CUSTOMER SATISFACTION, by Alan Dutka
WAS THERE A PEPSI GENERATION BEFORE PEPSI DISCOVERED IT?, by Stanley C. Hollander and Richard Germain
BUSINESS TO BUSINESS COMMUNICATIONS HANDBOOK, by Fred Messner
MANAGING SALES LEADS: HOW TO TURN EVERY PROSPECT INTO A CUSTOMER, by Robert Donath, Richard Crocker, Carol Dixon and James Obermeyer
AMA MARKETING TOOLBOX (SERIES), by David Parmerlee
AMA COMPLETE GUIDE TO SMALL BUSINESS MARKETING, by Kenneth J. Cook
AMA COMPLETE GUIDE TO STRATEGIC PLANNING FOR SMALL BUSINESS, by Kenneth J. Cook
AMA COMPLETE GUIDE TO SMALL BUSINESS ADVERTISING, by Joe Vitale
HOW TO GET THE MOST OUT OF TRADE SHOWS, by Steve Miller
HOW TO GET THE MOST OUT OF SALES MEETINGS, by James Dance
STRATEGIC MARKET PLANNING, by Robert J. Hamper and L. Sue Baugh

For further information or a current catalog, write:
NTC Business Books
a division of *NTC Publishing Group*
4255 West Touhy Avenue
Lincolnwood, Illinois 60646–1975 U.S.A.